Are

From

Cyberspace

St. Martin's Griffin

New York

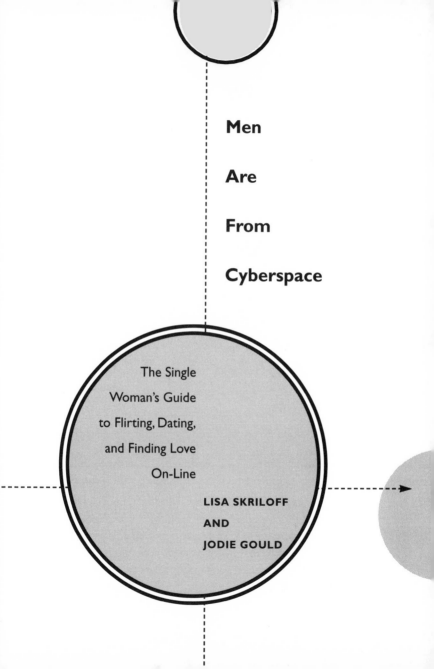

Men

Are

From

Cyberspace

The Single
Woman's Guide
to Flirting, Dating,
and Finding Love
On-Line

LISA SKRILOFF

AND

JODIE GOULD

Design by Songhee Kim

Library of Congress Cataloging-in-Publication Data

Skriloff, Lisa.
    Men are from cyberspace : the single woman's guide to flirting, dating, and finding love on-line / Lisa Skriloff and Jodie Gould.   —
1st ed.
      p. cm.
     ISBN 0-312-17105-6
     1. Man-woman relationships—Computer network resources.
   2. Electronic-mail messages.   3. Computer sex.   4. Internet (Computer   network)—Social aspects.   5. On-line chat groups.
   I. Gould, Jodie.   II. Title.
   HQ801.S597   1997
   025.06'3067—dc21   97-4395
                                                 CIP

First St. Martin's Griffin Edition: December 1997

10 9 8 7 6 5 4 3 2 1

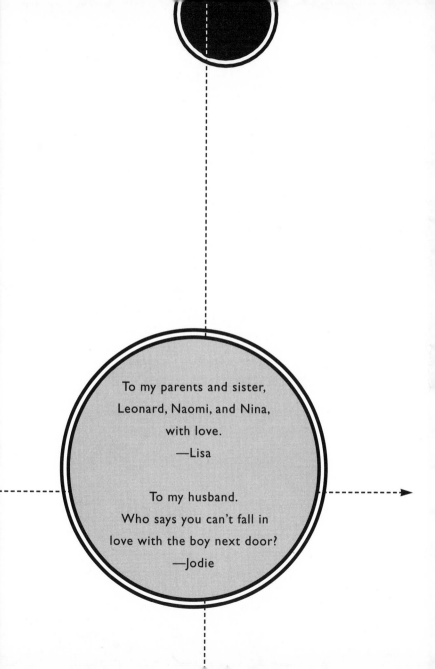

To my parents and sister,
Leonard, Naomi, and Nina,
with love.
—Lisa

To my husband.
Who says you can't fall in
love with the boy next door?
—Jodie

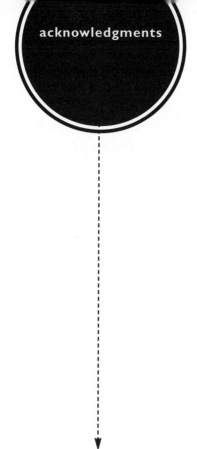

acknowledgments

We would like to thank our friend and agent Linda Konner for her creativity, savvy, and perseverance. Our thanks also to Kelley Ragland of St. Martin's for her editorial skills and enthusiasm, and to the following people for their invaluable assistance: Leonard Skriloff, Aliza Sherman of Webgrrls, Carol Wallace of Prodigy, Carole and Bill Hinners of Prodigy Singles, Trish McDermott of Match.com, Nora Contini of Jewish Community Online, and Daniel Bender of Cupid's Network/American Singles. Finally, our heartfelt appreciation to all the cyberdaters who shared their stories with us. May romance continue to flourish on-line and off.

contents

Men

Are

From

Cyberspace

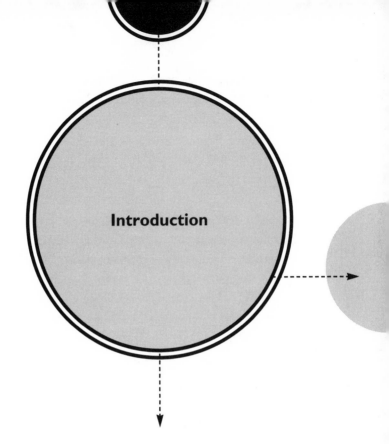

Introduction

We're not psychologists, social workers, or celebs. You've heard enough advice from them. (Gee, I wonder if Pamela Anderson Lee has any great tips on finding men?) We're just two twenty-first-century gals who have discovered a huge reservoir of available men and we want to share the wealth. That's right. Men *are* from cyberspace!

Why is the Internet fast replacing bars, bookstores, and

malls as a woman's venue of choice for meeting men? There are 40 million people currently on-line from 160 countries, and 70 percent of these Internet users are men! That's what we call great odds if you're a single woman.

Intelligent, creative, and worldly men from all over the globe are using the computer to woo single women, vying for their conversation, affection, and phone numbers. (There are also geeks and freaks, and we will tell you how to avoid them later.) No smoky rooms, loud music, or other distractions.

But how does a woman looking for more than an on-screen relationship make the transition from virtual reality to flesh-and-blood reality? That's where *Men Are from Cyberspace: The Single Woman's Guide to Flirting, Dating, and Finding Love On-Line* comes in. This book will show you how to navigate your way through cyberspace to a busier social life and, from there, to wherever you'd like: a short-and-sweet fling or possibly an engagement ring.

Men Are from Cyberspace offers firsthand reviews of the on-line dating sites, success stories of dates and mates found on-line, dating Netiquette, a glossary of cyberterms, advice on how to avoid the perverts and scam artists, and tips on how to engage in mind-blowing cybersex—a warm-up for the real thing.

We have also included the best on-line places to find single men interested in romance, the best way to join the chat rooms if you're a "newbie" (cybervirgin), and information on how to interpret the graphic symbols that men often use. We will tell you the funniest and sometimes embarrassing true stories about digital dating (most real and screen names have been changed, so don't try E-mailing any of the people in this book), and give you tips on how to go from E-mail to real male, from chat room to groom, from mouse to spouse—well, you get the idea.

Even though the Internet may seem daunting at first, we will show you how easy it is to discover where the cyberbeaus are. For those of you who have yet to cruise the Net, imagine you just walked into a bar and are instantly surrounded by a half-dozen guys armed with their best pickup lines. You ask them each a question, and decide which one you would like to talk to. You chat for a while until you're either bored, turned off, or turned on, at which point you can go someplace a little more private with the guy you just met or choose another bachelor. By this time, three or four new guys have eagerly approached you.

Sound like a fantasy? It happens nearly every time a woman enters an on-line chat room. With a computer, a modem, and a little guidance about where to click, you too can be typeface-to-typeface with men who are looking for—and dreaming about—you! But do keep in mind that cyberdating is not a substitute for the real thing. Cyberdating is just another way to make new friends and meet new people. If one of those new friends turns into a boyfriend or husband, all the better.

Our experience has been that you will find the same dating problems on-line that you do in the real world. There are jerks, nerds, pervs, hackers, slackers, and crazies. But there are also smart, romantic, relationship-seeking, heart-throbbing men out there. Why not use our God-given technology for the greater good of womankind?

And if you're a dyed-in-the-modem cybernymph, we'll give a list of some of the hottest sex sites around (at last count there were 5,000 on AOL alone). Of course, like any dating experience, women must be careful about who they meet on-line. The nature of this electronic beast makes it both an intimate and impersonal medium. For starters, you can't always tell if the man you're chatting with is (a) actually a man, (b) the spitting image of Brad Pitt, as he described, or (c) wearing a wedding ring.

We will discuss the hot-button issue of on-line fidelity. Is it really cheating if you haven't actually reached out and touched someone in real life? The jury is still out about whether cybersex with someone other than your spouse is grounds for divorce. We'll tell you about one husband who filed for divorce after reading his wife's sexy E-mail exchanges with a man she'd been cyberdating, and another who killed his cybercheating wife in a jealous rage.

We also provide tips on how to protect yourself from stalkers and other potentially dangerous types. Although cyberdating is safe when done correctly, there have been incidents where women were physically attacked by someone they met and "dated" on-line. All this can put a woman at risk for her safety, not to mention a broken heart or a broken vow.

We have answered as many FAQs (cyberlingo for "Frequently Asked Questions") as we can. If you have more questions after reading this book (and you will), or if you would like to share your cyberdating experiences, *fe*-mail us at MenRfrom@aol.com. We are forever interactive and we want to hear from you.

The bottom line is that the Internet opens up a whole new frontier for meeting men by bringing eligible bachelors from all over the world right into your bedroom or office (and you don't even have to wear makeup to entertain them)! Just sign on and let your fingers do the talking. Whether it's a boyfriend, husband, or 'puter pal you want, *Men Are from Cyberspace* will be your compass as you launch into cyberspace. Happy landings!

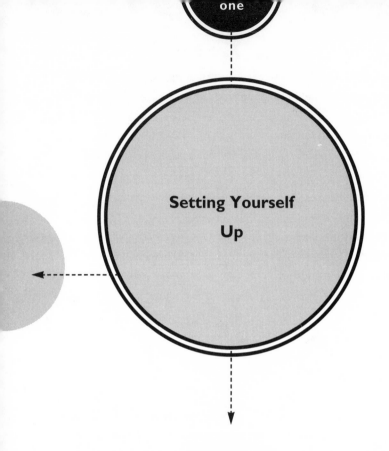

one

Setting Yourself Up

THE BIG THREE

We are going to assume that you already own a computer, so we won't go over the boring details about equipment and the PC versus Mac debate. To each her own computer. If you want to know more about the technical stuff, ask a guy when you're next on-line; guys love talking about computers and especially love to offer their opinions about what kind of computer to buy.

In the old days, guys would talk about sports and cars in the same rhapsodic way that they now discuss computers. Nowadays, the question, "How big is your hard drive?" has replaced, "What kind of car do you drive?" Many women are also into computers, which is great, because the more you know, the more fun you can have with them. (It won't hurt you professionally either.)

We will refer throughout the book to at least one of the Big Three commercial on-line services: America Online (AOL), Prodigy, and CompuServe. These services are available through subscription only, and they all provide access to the entire Internet. The Big Three phone companies (AT&T, MCI, and Sprint) also offer on-line service connections, but have yet to enter the chat room and romance business.

America Online (800-4-ONLINE) is the largest commercial on-line service with more than 6 million subscribers. Its size has created some large-scale problems with people unable to sign on at certain times. But it does offer the widest selection of romance sites, chat rooms, bulletin boards, and special forums for singles.

CompuServe (800-848-8199) is the second largest with more than 4 million members, but it's targeted to business types and has only a few romance features for singles. It does offer tons of special-interest bulletin boards, newsgroups, games, and a chat area for live conversations. This service has a large international membership, so if you're looking for love outside the U.S. borders, you might want to choose CompuServe.

Prodigy (800-776-3449) has just 1.5 million members, but it is extremely romance-friendly. You can also connect to Prodigy through the Internet, rather than dialing the on-line service directly.

In addition to the Big Three, you can get on-line through the Microsoft Network (800-373-3696), which you automatically receive with Windows 95 or better. It is connected to the MSNBC television network, but it's still in its infancy, so romance-seekers should probably invest in one of the more established commercial services.

There are also Internet Service Providers (ISPs), which are different from the commercial services in that they provide only E-mail service and Internet access. The great thing about ISPs, though, are the low monthly fees and unlimited access to the Web at no extra cost. You can always get an ISP in addition to one of the Big Three.

Ask friends to suggest an ISP in your area, or, if you have access to the Web via AOL, go to www.thelist.com/ for a listing of ISPs by state and area code. When you find one in your town or city, call and ask about their low-cost plans. Don't forget to ask about technical support as well.

Now that you're launched, let's get down to the serious business of finding love in cyberspace.

There are so many people on-line. How can I stand out among all the other women in cyberspace?

Your member profile and screen name(s) are your major calling cards. They give you the chance to create an on-line personality, or more than one. On AOL, you can select up to five screen names and profiles. This gives you the opportunity to tap into the "Sybil" inside all of us. Sometimes you're in the mood for intelligent conversation; sometimes you just want to get down and dirty. (Yes, some women like to talk sexy, too.)

Creating a profile is the Internet equivalent of wearing a negligee or your prep-school pleats. When you sign on, you can choose the personality you want to display that day. Here's what Lisa has in her AOL profile:

Screen name:	SrtaLisa (Señorita Lisa)
Member name:	Lisa S.
Location:	New York City, NY USA
Birth date:	Gemini
Sex:	Female
Marital status:	Single
Computer:	Power Mac
Hobbies:	Spanish, movies, traveling, media junkie, scuba diving
Occupation:	Writer

Quote: Who can take a nothing day and
              suddenly make it all seem worth-
              while?

Sometimes the screen name you've chosen has already been taken, so you'll have to come up with another one. In any case, be creative and original. To reveal Lisa's interest in scuba diving, she tried the screen name SharkBait, but it was taken. So she tried Mermaid instead. Both are kind of sexy and convey info about her love of the sea. Lisa now uses five screen names at different times depending on her mood or intention.

SrtaLisa is the name she uses most often when she feels like talking to men. Since Srta is short for Señorita, it tells the guy that Lisa speaks Spanish. It shows that she is female without being too risqué. (A name like Candy4U would provoke an entirely different response.)

Lisa had the following conversation with a man from Italy who sent her a message after seeing her SrtaLisa screen name:

> Synesisl: I bet you are from Spain?
> SrtaLisa: No, but I speak Spanish. And you?
> Synesisl: A little of everything.
> SrtaLisa: Where are you from?
> Synesisl: Italy!
> SrtaLisa: Do you live in Italy?

Synesisl: Yes. In Bari.

SrtaLisa: Are you in Italy right now?

Synesisl: Yes! I am using the World Wide Web.

SrtaLisa: My very first international message! I have been to Bari and Brindisi to take the ferry to Corfu.

Synesisl: Listen, I don't know when I will be able to be connected again . . . and if I will be connected to you. But if you travel to Bari again, you can leave a message with Franco at the Airport of Palese. He will know where I will be at the time.

Sometimes Lisa uses her screen name, PrfctBound (short for perfect bound), which has publishing as well as sexy connotations. This lets her save SrtaLisa for her more demure persona. She wanted to attract literary types with a good sense of humor. She did meet the editor of a city magazine this way. He used a computer flower to pick her up. It worked:

MOE33: @}--->----- A flower for you.

PrfctBound: Gee, thanks. I love it.

MOE33: You're welcome. I was just giving up hope of your returning my message.

MOE33: Great name, by the way.

PrfctBound: You get it!

MOE33: I'm a magazine editor, I better.

PrfctBound: I was hoping a sexy guy in publishing
             would notice!

MOE33:   \<blush\>.

Then later . . .

Moe33:   Would you like to get naked with me?

PrfctBound: That was fast . . . what happened to
             \<blush\>?

Moe33:   I was blushing the whole time I asked.

As these examples show, to stand out among all the other cybergals, it's important to choose your screen name (and develop your profile) with the same care that you would use in deciding what to wear on a real-life date.

How important is the personal quote?

Some member profiles and romance Web sites give you the opportunity to select a personal quotation. The personal quote is just another insight into your character and personality. It can also provide the launching pad for a discussion when you first meet on-line.

When choosing a personal quote, you can be provocative, poetic, or witty (it helps if you're naturally funny). By choosing a line from the theme song of *The Mary Tyler Moore Show* ("Who can turn the world on with her smile?") for one of her screen names, Lisa was greeted by men who were also fans of the show.

One fellow from London who was not familiar with the TV theme song thought it was a quaint expression of her sunny outlook on life, so you might want to consider a more universal quote if your search goes beyond the cultural boundaries of North America. Avoid using cliches such as "Let a smile be your umbrella." Think image. Think sexy. Think smart. You can also choose a line from your favorite film, song, author, or pundit.

For PrfctBound, Lisa chose the quote, "You know how to whistle, don't you?" She attracts intelligent, classic-movie fans with that one. Some know how to finish the phrase with, "You just put your lips together and blow." Those are the guys who get a response.

Following are some sample quotes (good and bad).

Good Quotes
Fall seven times, stand up eight.
Life's a banquet and most poor fools are on a diet.
You can't get enough of what you don't really want.
Always remember you're unique, just like everyone else.
Okay, who stopped the payment on my reality check?
Time is the best teacher; unfortunately it kills all its students.

Morbid Quotes
Life's a bitch and then you die.
We're all in this alone.
It's as BAD as you think, and they ARE out to get you.

Infantile Quotes

When the cat's away, this mouse does play!

Cum on over and join in the fun.

I have what you want right here on my laptop.

Hostile Quotes

Life's a bitch, but God forbid she divorces me.

A woman without a man is like a fish without a bicycle.

I used to wake up grumpy; other times I let her sleep.

Meaningless-Cliched Quotes

What, me worry?

Life is too short.

People with life insurance don't die.

Quotes That Go on Too Long

The hottest places in hell are reserved for those who, when in times of great moral crisis, chose to remain silent.

Braggart Quotes

I can please u. I'm not the 20-minute man. One hour or more. NO BS. WANT WOMEN WHO CAN GO THE DISTANCE.

What's the best way to pick up a guy on-line?

It depends on what you're looking for. If it's cybersex you want, go into any romance room, where you'll find plenty of horny men. As a woman, you will be immediately surrounded by guys vying for your attention. Like strutting peacocks, they will try to win you over with their best lines of prose. Choose the guy who strikes your fancy, and go into a private room. Start with some verbal foreplay and let your imagination and fingers run wild!

If it's a serious relationship you're looking for, go into a member-created chat room with a topic that interests you. Forget about the guys who open with, "pussy wet?" If he's only interested in cybersex, you'll soon know. On the other hand, if he asks what you look like (though ideally, that question should be asked much later in the conversation), and you say, "I'm a tall, blonde knockout with double Ds, and I don't mean my grades," then you are the one taking the chat in another direction.

If you're in a chat room on AOL, maybe having a conversation, maybe just "lurking" (hanging out without participating), you'll hear a little chime as if Tinkerbell had just flown in. A box appears on your screen with the name of a guy and his private greeting. This is called an IM or Instant Message. (After doing this for a while, you'll notice that IM really means "Instant Men.") This is a private message that can't be seen by the rest of the room. You can also initiate a conversation with a guy by sending *him* a private message.

As soon as you meet a guy who seems nice, check his member profile. This will give you some ideas for subjects to talk about. It could be something about where he lives—"Oh, I'm from New York, too"—or about his hobbies, or about the quote he selected. If his quote says, "I'm still the master of my domain," you can have a chat about the latest *Seinfeld* episode. Plus, you don't have to knock yourself out being clever (although it's great if you are) because *he's* the one who's courting you.

Next, you'll have a conversation where you learn more about the guy and you reveal a little bit about yourself. After a while, you might sign off and arrange for a time to chat again on-line. Whether you are being picked up or doing the trolling, make sure you open the chat with lines that will reel them in, instead of making them jump out of the tank.

The Best (and Worst) Pickup Lines
The following are some real on-line examples.

Bad Openers
How old are you?
Are you horny?
Do you like big-breasted women?
How big is your wallet?
Stop looking. You've found the man you were lookin' for.
What do you look like?

Better Openers

This is my first time on-line. Be gentle.

I see you're an ad man. Sell me on you!

What do you think about what happened on *X-Files* last night?

I'm a dog owner, too. What kind of dog do you have?

Want to chat with a fellow skier?

I really admire you.

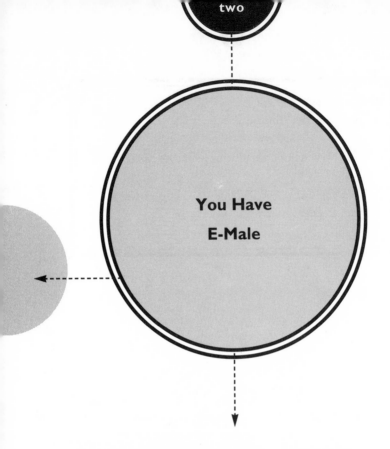

two

**You Have
E-Male**

FINDING AND MEETING GUYS ON-LINE

One of the best places to meet men on-line are in the chat rooms, a location on a commercial service or Web site where strangers are in live communication with one another. It's like talking on the phone, only you are *reading* what the other person is saying. You can read the whole conversation and join in with your own comments, or just lurk. It's usually better to lurk before you leap so you can get the feel of the room or the thread of the conversation before jumping in.

Even better are the newsgroups (or discussion groups), a network of bulletin boards that provide special-interest forums on everything from the Bible to *The X-Files*. They are without a doubt the coolest thing about the Net. Some newsgroups have an administrator who selects which messages get posted and which get spiked. Others are supervised by the participants themselves.

There are more than 20,000 newsgroups on the Usenet system, and some of the most popular ones have tens of thousands of readers who log on regularly to check out the latest info on their favorite field, hobby, political, or sexual bent. (See Chapter 11, Becoming a Newsgroupie, for a sample listing.)

What's the deal with the chat rooms? Where are the good ones?

Here's the deal: Most of the chat rooms created by the larger on-line services such as AOL are lame, and the people who gather there are *BORING*. If you're new at chat-room chatter, visit the New Member Lounge to get your feet wet. Then, check out the best chat rooms, which are the ones created by the members themselves. You will eventually discover which ones are your favorites and begin to recognize the cast of characters who inhabit them (or become a character yourself). The nice thing about frequenting a chat room is that it becomes like a local hangout, an on-line "Cheers," if you will, where everybody knows your name—screen name, that is.

Each service has a different way to access chat rooms. On AOL, for example, you start at the Main Menu and click onto People Connection. That will bring you into a chat room immediately. This is the "lobby." The box at the top of the screen tells you how many people are in the room (the maximum is twenty-three). It also tells you the names of the people who just entered the room (including yours). On Prodigy, you can JUMP to "chat" before you even sign on, and you'll be placed immediately at the entrance to the chat facility. A few more clicks and you're in. On CompuServe the magic word is GO.

Once you're in a chat room, you can lurk, join in the conversation, check member profiles to see who's interesting enough to send a private message to, or go into other rooms to see what's happening there.

To check out the other "official" rooms in AOL, click on Public Rooms and scroll down the list of categories and topics such as News, Sports, and Finance; Romance; Over Forty; Arts and Entertainment; Teen Chat; or Thirtysomething. You'll also see a box labeled Member Rooms. If you click on there, you'll be able to see the list of topics that were created by other on-line members.

Since your goal is to find a date, you might want to pick the room with your geographic location such as Virginians Online or NYC Room. If there isn't one, you can start one.

Some member rooms have a sexual theme such as Hopelessly Romantic or Cross-Dressers. There are also plenty of places to find fellow hobby enthusiasts such as bladers or runners, and later on we'll tell you where.

Members Only

Since many chat rooms are started by members, new ones are constantly being added. The following are a few recently spotted member chat rooms on AOL:

Physicians Online

Jock Dorm

Millionaires Lounge

Blondes

Buxom Women

Lonely Housewives

Trailer Park Trash

Cops Who Flirt

Alone in the Office at Midnight

Chateau Dungeon

So Fla Bi Wives (Southern Florida Bisexual Wives)

How do I find the newsgroup that's right for me?

If you are on AOL, you can use the "search all newsgroups" button on the main screen and type in your topic of interest. This will give you all the newsgroups available on AOL, though not all of the newsgroups available on the Net (as a protection to minors). If you want to find those, you need to know the name of the newsgroup in order to access it. (For CompuServe, Go: Newsgroups; Prodigy, Jump: Newsgroups.)

Newsgroups are organized by categories or topics called hierarchies. The newsgroup will break down its content from left to right. For example, alt.binaries.pictures.personal is a specific newsgroup that allows you to exchange pictures with other users.

"Alt" stands for alternative groups. Although this does *not* mean alternative (deviant) topics, there are more than enough sexually oriented newsgroups, if that's what you're looking for. But the entire alt.* listing also contains newsgroups for your favorite musical artist as well as your most fervent social or political issue.

If you search "personals," you will get all the newsgroups where you can post or browse the personal ads. Newsgroups for personal ads and finding love include the following, but see our list on pages 149–152 for more:

- alt.personals
- alt.personals.ads
- alt.sex.wanted

You can further narrow your search for a cyberbeau by going to local groups such as "yourcity*" or "yourorg*" (i.e., New York.coffee.bars).

Like any chat room, the more you visit and post on a newsgroup, the faster you will become known to the group. When this happens, you will probably start corresponding with some of the guys who have also posted there. You can also check the postings for a brilliant, insightful comment, then E-mail the Einstein directly with a comment of your own, or just a note to say how much you liked his posting. This is guaranteed to get you a response.

Are there any nice guys out there? I want to meet someone on-line, but I'm afraid that all the men in cyberspace are geeks or pathetic freaks.

Your fears are unfounded. There are so many men in cyberspace now that it is grossly unfair to write them all off as a bunch of computer wonks and nerds. (Lisa happens to fancy the Bill Gates type anyway. Who wouldn't like a brilliant billionaire?) The fact is, cyberspace is filled with doctors, lawyers, artists, actors, and a whole host of sexy, fascinating men and women. However, if you are on nerd alert, you can weed out guys you aren't interested in by their E-mail and, if it gets that far, over the phone.

A Girl's Guide to Geek Guys

We found this list of "Why Geeks Rule" in a *Hotwired* magazine article by Mikki Halpin and Victoria Maat. (Both are obviously geek-magnets, but what living, breathing woman isn't?)

A Girl's Guide to Geek Guys (Cont.)

- They're smart.
- They are generally available.
- They can fix things.
- Your parents will love them.

And some of our own reasons . . .

- They're likely to be employed after college.
- They won't cheat on you unless, of course, Steve Jobs suddenly becomes available.
- You won't be a sports widow, and COMDEX (a large computer trade show) only comes around once a year.

I played tennis last week with a guy I'd really like to get to know better. He gave me his business card with his E-mail address on it. Should I send him a message?

Why not? He wouldn't have given you his card unless he wanted you to do something with it. E-mail can be used by women as a way of initiating contact without being too forward, or actually picking up the telephone.

Why not send him an E-mail about a Web site that is for tennis lovers? This way he'll know you're interested, and you can stay in touch in between tennis dates. Let him make the next move, however. You served the ball, it's his turn to lob it back into your court.

How do I know if I'm going to hit it off with a guy I've met on-line?

You don't. But if you never progress beyond electronic communication, you'll never know, will you? If you like each other on-line, talk on the phone. If you don't like his voice or manner, say, "I'm sorry, I don't think this is going to work out, but it was nice talking to you." End of story.

Won't guys think I'm desperate lurking around for men on-line?

That's the beauty of romancing the Net. It's a party line, mall, church social, club, and classroom rolled up into one virtual ball. People go on-line for so many different reasons, and your signing on does not necessarily mean you're trolling for men (even if you are). You could be Networking or Netplaying.

Either way, it shouldn't matter what anyone else thinks, especially a virtual stranger. No one who's looking for love should be considered "desperate." It's a basic need, and a man who thinks otherwise can just get over himself. And, as we've mentioned before, you won't have to make the first move when you're, say, entering a chat room. Men will seek you out because you are a single woman.

I'm really attracted to men who ride motorcycles. Is there somebody out there for me? (P.S. I'm on AOL.)

Yeah, he's out there and finding him is easy. Try searching the member directory for Keyword: Harley. That's basically what dating services do—they try to hook you up with like-minded men in your geographic area. The more targeted the reference, the more likely you will be to make a match.

If a guy cares enough to write "Harleys Rule" in his personal quote or profile, he may be thrilled to hear from a biker chick. Don't try to locate him on-line and send him an instant message, however. That's a little too forward. Instead, write him a short, lighthearted, E-mail message saying, "Hey, I see you ride a Harley. I've always wanted to hop on the backseat. Got any room on yours?"

What's the best time to go on-line to meet guys?

Surprise, surprise, Friday nights are usually hoppin' with singles. Saturday nights are also busy, but not as hectic as Fridays. (The Neilsen ratings people found that the most on-line activity occurs between 7:00 P.M. and 10:00 P.M. You might find it difficult to get on-line at these peak times, or that many of the chat rooms are full to capacity. Twenty-three is the max in AOL; not because it's a fire hazard, but because it's difficult to maintain a conversation with more than twenty-three people at once.

If you enjoy a mosh pit of chat, a CompuServe channel can have more than one hundred people in one room, but it could take forty lines before you get a response to your comment. Keep trying. Once you're in a room, you'll probably get more requests to go private than you'll know what to do with.

Late nights are also a good time to get wired, or to wind down after work. Most people (not us, but most people) work at an office, so afternoons will bring a clear line of writers, actors, artists, and the self-employed.

Are guys on-line any smarter than the ones I'd meet in a bar?

Not necessarily. Nowadays just about everyone owns a computer, so it's not just an exclusive club of M.I.T. graduates out there. Once you've been on-line for a while, you'll be appalled by the number of illiterates you'll encounter. (Hint to everyone on-line: Keep Mr. Webster nearby at all times.)

However, if it's brains you're looking for, the Net can help you zero in on the Men-sas, and gives people who are verbally endowed an opportunity to show off their bantering skills. (If you don't know what Mensa is, you're not one, so move on to the next question.)

Try typing (search word): Mensa and see what you find. There is sure to be a group somewhere on the Web. In this case, casting a wide Net is not always as effective as narrowing your search. You can also try taking out a personal ad (see Chapter 8, From Click to Tom, Dick, and Harry), making sure to write "intelligence" as one of the important traits you're looking for in a man. Also, newsgroups and chat rooms that discuss politics and social issues will attract the serious-minded folk.

Sandee Brawarsky, author of *How to Meet Men as Smart as You,* told us, "The Internet opens up great possibilities for meeting smart men—and women. When you're correspond-ing on-line, wit and intelligence shine through brightly."

Are you more likely to "click" with someone you've met on-line?

Again, this is an area in which virtual reality and reality are about the same. A friend of ours named Wendy found that half the dates she met through the computer were great and half were duds. She remembers how her heart fluttered madly after meeting one handsome writer whom she had met on the Net for cappuccino. The virtual roses he sent her were matched stem for stem with the real ones.

She will also never forget how one guy whom she met for the first time wore thigh-hugging, butt-padding bicycle shorts. A jerk is a jerk is a jerk, no matter where you've met him. But clicking your mouse wisely will get you more dates than you ever thought possible. And the more you date, the greater your odds of finding your true love.

I want to get married now! What can I do on-line to speed up the process?

Okay, so you're starting to get the shakes about not being married. Before we tell you how to get the wedding wheels in motion, remember that marriage does not necessarily mean happiness. (Why do you think the divorce rate is still 50 per-cent? Some people are living unhappily ever after.) Instead, your goal should be finding someone who you could envision sharing your life (and bathroom) with. Should that happen, you can throw an expensive party attended by friends and relatives you don't even know or like.

That said, we suggest that you skip the chat room/news-group route and go directly to the personals. (Flip to Chapter 8, From Click to Tom, Dick, and Harry, for personals available on-line.) Match.com, for example, has a question in its profile form about your goals for meeting someone. For some it will be "to make new E-mail friends" or "to meet someone for fun and romantic interludes." For you, it will be "looking for a serious relationship that could lead to marriage." You can also search the profiles for those guys who are equally marriage-minded.

After that, don't mention the "M" word again for a while. Since the guy you're meeting for a date has already read your profile, he knows that you are looking for a husband. There's no need to bring up the topic again until you've established that you two might be getting serious. Even if you're lighting a candle every night to Aphrodite, the goddess of love, praying that tomorrow you will meet your future hubby, do not let your desperation seep into your cyber-conversation any more than you would in real-life conversation. Have fun. Enjoy your dates. Worry about the legal contracts later.

If you absolutely hate the idea of taking out a personal ad, then you can use your E-mail or private room chats as a screening process. It's much easier to ask personal questions on-line than it is in person. "Have you ever been married?" is a common way to introduce the topic and to get an idea about his feelings on the subject. If he says, "Ugh, yes. Two disasters, one near miss," the red flag should go up. If he says, "No, but I'd like to someday," he may be someone worth getting to know.

I'm over 50, and I wasn't weaned on computers. Are there any men my age out there and will they be interested in a cybersenior?

At fifty-plus, you are far from a cybersenior. And you no longer need a degree in computer science to enjoy the fruits of the Net. You and millions of other Baby Boomers are doing just that. The Big Three service providers all have chat rooms and newsgroups for the Baby Boomer set. AOL has a Fifty-something chat room, as well as a SeniorNet for people in their sixties and seventies. If you're divorced, there are support groups for divorcees (gay and straight). Exactly what do you have to lose by exploring for men your own age? Seek and ye shall find. (Check out Bonnie's love story in Chapter 9, From Mouse to Spouse.)

Are role-playing games a good way to meet guys?

We have heard of couples who have met and fallen in love while playing a fantasy game on GEnie. We also heard from a woman who complained that her (now ex) husband, whom she met playing a fantasy game, could not stop having cyber-sex even after they were married. He was addicted to fantasy, she said.

If games are your thing, however, there are casino games, chess, checkers, backgammon, and trivia as well as Multi-User

Dungeon (MUD), Multi-User Shared Hallucination (MUSH), and Multi-User Object-Oriented (MOO) sites.

The problem with most game areas is that although they are interactive and give you the opportunity to meet people, you have no control over who you play with. Most of them are on a first-come, first-play basis. Although interactive games aren't our first choice for meeting a mate, you may find them intellectually stimulating and exciting. Look for one in your area that has recurring characters. For example, one group of New Yorkers who meet regularly in a virtual soap opera also meet regularly in real life.

For more info on MUDs and other games, check out the FAQs (answers to the most Frequently Asked Questions) at www.cis.ohiostate.edu/hypertext/faw/usenet/games/mudfaq/top.html. The ImagiNation Network, a subscription service from AT&T (www.att.com/truechoice/imagra2.html) is another place where game-playing couples have romped. For free virtual-reality chat rooms, see www.thepalace.com.

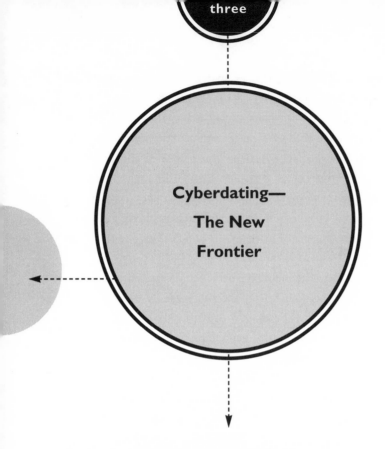

three

Cyberdating—
The New
Frontier

ROMANCE IN THE NEW MILLENNIUM

You've heard it before and you will hear it from now until the next century—we are entering the new millennium. What this means, aside from one hell of an excuse for a blowout New Year's party, is that many of the dating rules have changed. We are pioneers of a sort, riding on our dust-covered computers, into the new frontier. Here are a few tips to help you on your journey.

Are men in cyberspace really only interested in sex?

Although sex is definitely in the hearts and on the minds of many cybermen, we'd have to say that you will find many men (depending on their age, marital status, and level of maturity) who are interested in other things. The reasons men are in cyberspace are as varied as the reasons men go to parties, tennis matches, Club Med, or singles bars. They might be looking to meet a woman for a relationship or even marriage. The best way to avoid the lusty lads is to stay out of the sex-oriented chat rooms.

Go instead to the newsgroups or bulletin boards that reflect interests, hobbies, or attitudes similar to your own. If you find yourself being hit on by a pack of cyberwolves, politely bat your virtual eyes and say, "No sex chat, please," or "I don't do cyber."

I met a guy in a chat room who seems just my type. Should I send him an E-mail?

Sending an E-mail to a guy you don't know is the same as sending him a Hallmark card. Before you do it, ask yourself, "Would I feel comfortable calling this guy on the phone or writing him a letter?" If the answer is no, don't do it! He knows your E-mail address. If he's interested, he'll use it.

Guys can also use E-mail as a way to keep their distance. Once, Cindy asked a guy she met on-line for his phone number. Instead of giving it to her, he said, "I'm usually on-line.

You can try to find me there." Clearly, he did not want to take the relationship any further.

How do I know if I'm wasting my time with a guy on-line?

Don't drag out an on-line relationship for too long. After all, your goal is to actually meet the guy in person. If he doesn't return your E-mails, or if he doesn't want to give you his phone number after a few on-line dates, move on to someone else.

I've met this amazingly wonderful guy who lives in the same state and went to the same college! We totally connected on-line, and we spend every night together on-line and on the phone. We agreed to "take it slow," but what does this mean in the cyberworld? Are there rules about how many hours we should spend on-line and on the phone?

Although it's important to take things slow, it sounds as if the two of you have a lot in common, and could probably speed up the pace a bit. If you're spending that much time on-line and on the phone with each other, it's time for a real date. Be careful, however, about having expectations that are too high. Although you've "connected" electronically, there is still the hurdle of real-life clicking to be crossed. Keep your expectations low (you obviously have patience and willpower) and you will be either pleasantly surprised or not so terribly disappointed by what happens in real life.

Should I bother talking to a guy who doesn't live in my hometown?

It depends on what you're looking for. Lisa doesn't bother with guys who live in Arizona since her goal is to date someone now, not in three months when the airfares go down. Other people are willing to go to the other end of the earth to find a soul mate.

There are plenty of stories about cybermarriages that started as long-distance relationships. Be prepared for enormous phone bills (and remember that it's cheaper to talk on-line than it is on the phone), dry periods between visits, and time warp caused by trying to squeeze as much emotional closeness as you can into a week or weekend. And there's also the anxiety about whether your beau is staying faithful to you. (Is it "Absence makes the heart grow fonder" or "Out of sight out of mind"?)

If you're trolling for out-of-towners, you must be willing to pick up stakes for the man you love, or to have him do the same for you, should a match be made in cyberspace.

Is it a bad idea to reveal too much about yourself on-line?

The anonymity of cyberspace can lead to all-night gab sessions where you talk about everything that has happened to you since you left the womb. Resist the temptation to reveal too much about your personal life too soon. Amy, a thirty-year-old reporter, once told a sympathetic guy she met on-line that she had a nervous breakdown the year before. She never heard from him again. Wait until after you've established a real bond before exposing the skeletons in your closet.

Chatting on-line is one of the best ways to find out if you are compatible with another person, so you should certainly let him know about your hobbies, interests, pet peeves, political leanings, past marriages, work situation, and other stuff that defines what kind of person you are. If you're a practicing Catholic and grew up in a family of twelve kids, that says a lot about who you are.

On the other hand, as Amy, the reporter, learned, you might want to stay away from revealing something deeply personal such as your chronic depression or eating disorder. Barbara remembers chatting with one guy who told her in their conversation that he had to wear a colostomy bag. In this case, it would have been better had he waited for her to get to know other things about him before revealing his medical condition. She admits that it scared her off. However, if you have a serious condition, don't wait too long to reveal it. Feelings can be saved if the person being wooed bolts sooner rather than later.

Note: The Friends' Health Connection introduces people with similar illnesses, disabilities, or injuries. Members may meet by E-mail, phone, or snail mail (actual mail delivered by the post office). Call 1-800-48-FRIEND for more information.

Playing on a Level Field

One of the greatest stories about a match made in cyber-space appeared in a recent *New York Times* article by Lois Smith Brady. She wrote about how Stephen Feldman, who was confined to a wheelchair after a spinal-cord injury, found Cory Zacker, his wife and soul mate, through the Thirtysomething chat room on AOL.

"If I were to go to a party, I would obviously stand out, no pun intended," Stephen, a thirty-six-year-old song-writer, told the reporter. "But on-line you can lead with your personality. It's a level playing field."

After chatting about *Seinfield*, books, movies, and vari-ous topics of general interest, the two discovered that they both shared the same tastes and Manhattan neighborhood. They decided to meet at the local Barnes & Noble book-store for some coffee. With no aspirations toward romance, Stephen and Cory, a thirty-two-year-old film editor, talked for hours. When they parted, Stephen looked up at Cory and said, "You can kiss me good night now."

Love quickly blossomed and, a month later, the couple were making plans for their wedding. "The nice thing for both of us, or maybe just for me, was how quickly the wheelchair issue receded," Stephen said. "I fell in love with him," Cory said. "The chair was just the way he got around."

When is it time to take the on-line relationship to the next step?

Cyberdating has several stages: the virtual meeting, the chats, the E-mail messages, the voice conversations, and eventually a real-life, face-to-face meeting. If you feel you're ready for the next stage (and he is, too), you're probably ready.

We believe if you've had three good on-line conversations, it's time to progress to the second stage of your relationship—the telephone. If you're looking for a serious relationship, you need to know quickly if this guy is marriage material.

E-mailing is a great way to glean some personal information from a guy, because some men find it easier to reveal things about themselves when they are not face-to-face. It's also hard for a woman to ask intensely personal questions about what a man wants in life on a real-life date. Don't go to the telephone stage until you've gathered enough background information and you feel that you might be compatible.

If you're not in a rush to get married, or if you are juggling two or three other suitors, you might want to keep one relationship on-line until you've discovered if the other two are going anywhere. If the first one doesn't work out, you have another man waiting in the wings. It may sound cold, but this is serious cyberdating.

Friends without Faces

The following are lines from a poem that was written anonymously and published in Prodigy's Singles Newsletter.

> Why is it we share, the thoughts in our mind.
> With those we can't see, as though we were blind.
> The answer is simple, it's as clear as a bell.
> We all have our problems, and need someone to tell.
> We can't tell real people, but tell someone we must.
> So we turn to the 'puter, and to those we can trust.
> And though it is crazy, the truth still remains.
> They are friends without faces, and odd little names.

I'm not a great writer, but I'm terrific in person. How can I get a guy to look beyond my writing skills for the real me?

Be honest about it. Once you meet someone you like online, tell him, "I'm much better on the phone and in person than I am on-line" or "I have so many ideas about this subject that I can't write them here. Do you want to talk on the phone?" Get his phone number and call.

Lisa has sometimes said, "I'm sorry for the short note, but I'm so tired after working all day, I can't be articulate tonight. I promise to call you in the morning if you give me your phone number." Stay away from the IRCs (Interactive Relay Chats) where you really have to think on your feet.

Also, men love to talk about themselves. If you'd rather read than write, ask him some questions about his work, favorite hobby, childhood, a current event, whatever will start him prattling. This way you'll get lots of great information while remaining aloof and mysterious (a turn-on to some men). When both of your interests are piqued, he can get to know the real you in real life.

I met a guy on-line who lives far away and it gets really expensive to talk on the phone. What are some of the things we can do on-line together, aside from cybersex?

You can make a cyberdate. That is, arrange to meet your beau in a private chat room at an agreed upon time. A friend of ours who met her long-distance boyfriend on-line, and sees him almost every weekend, plans several cyberdates during the week. This helps keep the phone bill down.

If you want to socialize with others, meet your boyfriend in a public chat room. You can even adopt screen names that are somehow connected (DoBee and DontBee). That way people will know you're a couple and no one will try to pick up either of you.

Another great thing about virtual reality is that *you* create it. You can travel through the wires to any place that your little hearts and imaginations desire. Take a walk on the beach, describing the sound and size of the waves, and the wet sand as it squishes between your toes. Go mountain climbing, sail the Caribbean, take a hot-air balloon ride. (Save the date on hard copy so you can read it over again whenever you're feeling lonely.) Then make a plan to meet in person and recreate your dream date in real life.

I'm not a beast, but I'm not exactly Cindy Crawford either. Do guys expect a woman to put her photo on-line?

You don't have to, if you don't want to. There are so many more men than women on-line that you can wait until you establish a relationship with a guy before exchanging GIFs (Graphic Interchange Formats), the standard format for PCs. (The first time someone asked Lisa, "Gotta GIF for me?" she thought he had left out the T and was asking for a present.)

The fact is, guys will want to talk to you no matter what you look like because they can always make up their own fantasy and attach it to you. Plus, the beauty of meeting someone on-line is that the guy should first fall in love with the inside you, not the outside you.

Luckily, unless you have designed your own home page with photo (and given a guy your Internet address), a guy can't scope out your photo unless you send him one. If you do want to have photos available to send, there are commercial scanning companies that will do this for you. Check your on-line service to see if it will scan a photo for free and place it in the photo library.

But if a guy asks for your photo early on in the relationship, it's probably a bad sign. It's better to describe yourself by focusing on your best features (everybody has them). Your long, wavy locks, big blue eyes, or buns of steel. Any man worth his salt will overlook your imperfections. And Goddess knows, they're not all Johnny Depps.

I'm going nuts checking my E-mail to see if this guy has responded to my messages. I can't keep logging on and off all the time. Help!

Once upon a time, before answering machines, love-crazed women would sit by the phone waiting for the guy to call. Now, women are falling head over heels for the "You have mail" man. Yes, it's nuts, and so is obsessing about E-mail. But it's a woman's prerogative to obsess, so what's a cybergal to do?

If you're both on AOL, you can check to see if a guy has even read the mail you've sent him by clicking "status" in your mailbox. This will tell you if he's read your message and, if so, the time and date he opened his E-mail. Very cool feature. (Unfortunately, this doesn't work if you've met someone who is on another service.) If a guy hasn't read or responded to your E-mail in a while, it may say something about his lack of interest in a relationship.

Susan, a twenty-two-year-old graduate student from Michigan, once sent a boyfriend a love letter by E-mail the night before he left for a ski trip. He had told her that he was taking his Powerbook with him on vacation, so she knew he could check his E-mail if he wanted to. She never got a reply during the week he was away, but she could also see that he hadn't read her message. Susan was comforted to learn that her boy-friend's lack of response was due to being too busy on the slopes. Unfortunately, since he didn't check his E-mail until ten days after he returned home, she soon lost interest.

"I thought we had hit it off, so I was annoyed that he didn't bother to check to see if I'd sent E-mail," she said. "It certainly indicated that I was a lot more interested in a relationship than he was. But it wasn't as bad as if he'd read my message and blew me off."

You can also look into using FlashSessions, which is also available on AOL. FlashSessions allow you to have your computer automatically sign on, send and receive mail and attached files, and sign off. You can schedule them at regular intervals, and you don't even have to be there! You can program a FlashSession to sign on and retrieve your mail at night, or while you're at work. In the morning, or when you get home from work, all of your mail will be waiting for you in your in box.

Reasons Why He Never E-mailed Again:
1. "He" could be a "she."
2. He doesn't really have the body of Brad Pitt and the brains of Stephen Hawkings.
3. The same reason as IRL (in real life): He found someone else.

I've been E-mailing a guy for six weeks who I really like, but I'm not so attracted to his picture. Should I meet with him anyway?

Once again, this can fall into the giving-the-guy-a-chance category. If there is something in their physical type that you know you are not attracted to, such as he's a blue-eyed blond and you are gaga for dark hair and brown eyes, then don't bother. We are attracted to certain things and there's just no changing it.

However, if his hair's a little messy, or his smile's a little crooked, or he's not the Calvin Klein poster boy you had hoped for, meet the guy and see what he looks like in person before you give him the boot. First of all, most people don't photograph well. (Have you ever looked at a photo of yourself and cringed?) It's not fair to judge a person by his (or her) picture alone. Another thing to keep in mind is that often when we meet someone who is not classically handsome, his personality, intelligence, or spirit takes over and suddenly he is the sexiest man alive.

Joan Goldstein, who runs Conscious Singles Connection, a matchmaking service in New York, says the Net has an advantage over face-to-face encounters because it eliminates what she calls the "visual knockout" that can happen when you first meet someone. Joan answered a personal ad from a man who described himself as handsome, passionate, and new in town. They spoke on the phone and immediately clicked.

And when it came time to meet in person, here's what happened.

"The appointed day arrives, the doorman rings, and I go down in the elevator to meet him," Joan recalled. "The elevator door opens and standing there is a man who could have been a double for Bozo the Clown. What was left of his hair was frizzy, bright orange, and halfway out to forever. He was skinny (I'm not attracted to skinny men) and wearing a Mexican poncho type of thing. My heart sank, but I'm a polite person so I did not press 'door close.'

"We went for a walk and the conversation flow that had been so amazing on the computer and phone reasserted itself. We spent about five hours together that day, talking until it got dark. I fell in love and we lived together for three years (we eventually split because he wanted kids and I didn't). If I had seen his picture first, I would *never* have given him the time of day. Because we were able to connect *first* on a personal level, it provided the opening that love needed to find its way."

Oh my God, I sent a message in the heat of passion to this guy I'm cyberdating, and now I want to take it all back. What should I do?

Even though it's a federal crime to tamper with the U.S. Mail, AOL has this cool little feature called "unsend." Click on "check the mail you've sent" and see if he's read your message. If not, you can click the "unsend" box and ::poof:: it never happened.

I spend so much time on-line that my fingers start tapping in my sleep.

Are you logging on for hours at a time? Are you eating meals at your monitor? Are you checking your E-mail more than four times a day? Is your skin starting to take on the bluish hue of your screen saver? Hello! You're a cyberaddict.

We're all in favor of a busy social life, on-line and off-line, and we don't think there's anything wrong with substituting a night of sitcoms with a night of chatting with perspective beaus, but if your cyberworld is starting to interfere with your real world of friendships, family, work, and physical health, *shut off your computer.* (Lisa found that she was losing sleep by staying on-line until 2 A.M.)

If you can't go cold turkey, try setting your watch or alarm clock to go off after an hour. If you just can't stop, consider joining the Internet addiction mailing list. Send E-mail to listserv@netcom.com with a message "subscribe i-a-s-g"; or contact Interneters Anonymous at http://www.itw.com/~rscott/ia.html.

Either way, think about the reasons why you're spending so much time at the keyboard. Are you simply having fun chatting with all the guys you've met on-line? Are you working on getting to know a man better so you can take it to the next stage? Or are you afraid to get too close to anyone, so you're keeping all your relationships elusive?

Are You a Cyberaddict?

If you find yourself chatting like mad when you're on-line and clamming up when you meet a guy in person, you have become too dependent on your computer. You don't want to spend the rest of your days staring at those little fish on your screen saver.

The following top ten list of signs that you may be addicted to the Net has been circulating (where else?) on the Net:

10. You wake up at 3 A.M. to go to the bathroom and stop to check your E-mail on the way back to bed.

9. You get a tattoo that reads, "This body best viewed with Netscape Navigator 3.0 or higher."

8. You turn your modem off and get this awful empty feeling, like you've just pulled the plug on a loved one.

7. You say "You've got mail" every time you see a postal worker.

6. You spend half the plane trip with your laptop on your lap, and your child in the overhead compartment.

5. You decide to stay in college for an additional year or two, just for the free Internet access.

4. You laugh at people with 2,400-baud modems.

3. You start using smiles in your snail mail.

2. The last guy you picked up was a JPEG (a computer photo file).

> **Are You a Cyberaddict? (Cont.)**
>
> And the number one sign you're addicted to the Net . . .
>
> 1. Your hard drive crashes. You haven't logged on for two hours. You start to twitch. You pick up the phone and manually dial your ISP's access number. You try to hum to communicate with the modem . . . you succeed!
>
> If this sounds like you, we repeat: *Shut off your computer and get out of the house.*

I met a guy on-line who I really like. The problem is that he's admitted to me that he's bald. I don't know if I can be attracted to someone who's bald. What should I do?

For God's sake, meet the cue ball. You already know that you like him personally. Maybe you'll find that you can get past his follicles and find something else to admire about him physically. Besides, some bald guys can be sexy. Had you met His Hairlessness at a party rather than on the Net, you probably wouldn't have given him a second glance. But the computer gave him the opportunity to woo you, and it seemed to work. So give him a shot. If he still doesn't do it for you, move on.

My on-line boyfriend just broke up with me and I'm not over him yet. I keep searching for him every time I sign on. What should I do?

Give yourself a period of mourning. Throw a black cloth over your computer and spend some time with your girl-friends talking about what jerks men can be. Then get back on the horse, uh, we mean, on-line. Remember, the odds are in your favor.

Try placing a personal ad or visiting a new chat room or newsgroup. Whatever you do, don't go into the same chat room you met your ex in for a while. And for God's sake, stop trying to locate him every fifteen minutes. Let him go.

I heard something about a buddy list. Can't it be used to stalk someone on-line?

Yes it can! There are pros and cons to buddy lists and we'll tell you about both. The Buddy System (Keyword: Buddy) is a service provided by AOL that helps you locate and communicate with 'puter pals. You type in a list of screen names in any category you choose (family, friends, boyfriends, poker pals, etc.) and you are notified whenever your buds are on-line.

For example, if your cyberbeau is in a chat room, you will get a message that tells you where he is so you can send him a private message. This is a convenient way to keep track of your partner and saves you from doing a search.

The problem is, buddy lists can also be used as a semi-stalking device by a guy who wants to know where you are in cyberspace at all times. "I don't like it," says Lisa, "because if I sign on to check my E-mail and there are guys who are looking for me, I'll get private messages that I feel obligated to respond to."

Should this happen to you, use the block feature that can take you off *all* buddy lists or just certain ones. This could be especially useful after a severed relationship. You could also sign on with another screen name or change your old screen name entirely. It's the on-line equivalent to changing the locks on your door or getting an unlisted phone number.

Is it unromantic to send or receive a love note via E-mail?

Some people have the old-fashioned notion that love notes should be handwritten and sealed with a perfumed kiss. This is a lovely idea, but it is not the only way to send a missive of love. As far as love bytes are concerned, we'll take them any way we can get them.

There are many creative ways to send a love note via E-mail. Men often send E-mail roses to their Juliets (long-stemmed and sometimes by the dozen), which is even nicer when it is followed by the real thing.

If you are tongue-tied, or in this case, writer-blocked, about what to say in a love message, you can find some help by contacting www.nando.net.toys.cyrano.html, a Web site that will help you write a romantic note. (See Chapter 12, Ladies, Start Your Search Engines.)

About six months ago I met this guy on-line who lives in England. Since then, we've sent E-mail, love letters, and have spent hundreds of dollars in phone calls. I think I'm in love, but, since I haven't met him, how do I know my feelings are real?

You may be in love, but whether your love will last is another question entirely. Does your stomach get all fluttery when you see a message from him? Do you have trouble saying good-bye to each other when you're chatting on-line or on the phone? Do you feel as though you don't need to date or see anyone else as long as you have him?

If you answered yes to these questions, you are one lovesick little puppy. These feelings are certainly real. But you need to meet each other in person to take it to the next step. It's like flying—you have to get some mileage under your belt before you get your pilot's license. Spend some time with him, on your turf and on his, and see if this relationship gets off the ground.

I'm looking for a guy who likes to play tennis and go to the theater. Is he out there in cyberspace?

Yep. And the best way to find him is to look in a chat room that caters to tennis and theater buffs. On AOL go to Keyword: Playbill to discuss the latest plays or musicals. If you're looking to play doubles instead of singles (ha-ha), go to Keyword: GS Tennis or Net Game and you will enter the Tennis Forum.

For other sports enthusiasts, Keyword: Sports will bring up

hoops, hockey, martial arts, lacrosse, bowling, golf, cycling, and baseball. Keyword: Hobbies will bring up other areas of interest such as writing, boating, and so forth.

On Prodigy, look under Chat for the area or room that relates to your interest (windsurfing, pets, music, etc.). CompuServe has three thousand to choose from, so knock yourself out.

What's the deal with sound effects on-line? How do you use them?

It is possible to send and receive sound files while chatting with your pals on-line. Most Windows applications require .WAV files (called waves). When you see the prefix {S you know it's a sound file, which can be up- and downloaded just like other files. The newer PCs and Macs have built-in speakers and multimedia capabilities. If you don't have them, you might have to buy a soundboard or more speakers. (Most people use a SoundBlaster-compatible soundboard.)

On-line services also have libraries full of music and lines from old movies that you can download onto your computer. If you have a microphone, you can even record your own sounds and upload them to your friends. If you type {S giggle, for example, all the people who share your file will hear you giggling.

It all sounds a bit frivolous to us, but if you're into this kind of thing, it's yet another way to communicate and share with that special someone, especially if he's a techie.

> **Giving Good Voice Mail**
>
> With the right equipment you can bypass Ma Bell (or Pa
> Sprint or Uncle MCI) and have unlimited voice commu-
> nication with anyone anywhere on the planet who has
> compatible software. Check out www.freetel.com, a gratis,
> ad-supported service that allows you to speak to your be-
> loved with only the standard computer equipment, a sound
> card, and a microphone.
>
> Vocaltech (www.vocaltech.com/) charges a one-time fee
> of $30 and requires you to prearrange your Internet calls
> via E-mail, snail mail, or by telephone.
>
> For more info on Internet phones see www.www.
> emagic.com/ or www.von.com. For directory information
> on others who can access voice messages dial www.
> pulver.com/iphone/.

**Should I set up a home page so guys can get the vitals
on me before we date?**

For those of you who don't already know, home pages are
Web sites that give a thumbnail sketch of a person, place, or
business. Many women are developing their own home pages
these days, especially creative types with innate design ability
or the resources to hire someone to design it for them. Home
pages are still used mostly by businesses, but if you are so
inclined, go for it.

You can add your picture along with your (snappily written) bio that includes your hobbies. (Don't post your phone number and address. It's too risky.) Home pages are a bit like having your own personal ad, and might save you time in giving out the details to prospective suitors. In this sense, there's no place like a home page.

Contact your on-line service to see if they have a simple point-and-click program for creating a home page. If you want something fancier, there are page-creation programs that you can buy or get free on the Net. One such service, EZPAGE, costs about $4.95 a month to maintain a site.

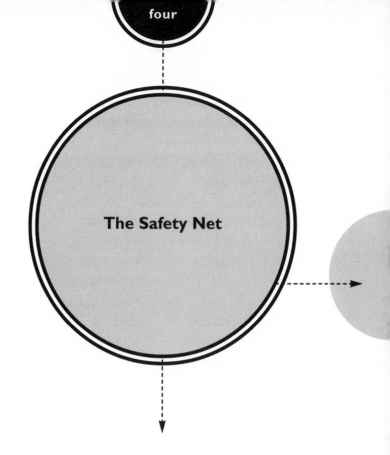

four

The Safety Net

ABSOLUTE MUSTS FOR PLAYING IT SAFE WHEN YOU'RE READY TO MEET IN REAL LIFE

If you're truly serious about finding a mate (and we know you are because you bought this book), your ultimate goal should be to meet your cyberbeau in real life (IRL). (A Netgirl cannot live by virtual love alone.) But to reach that goal, you must go through several stages of computer courtship.

Stage one: The virtual meeting. (Chat rooms, newsgroups, personals, etc.)

Stage two: Clicking. (Going private. Making regular cyberdates. Perhaps engaging in cybersex.)

Stage three: Calling. (As in speaking on the telephone. Perhaps engaging in phone sex.)

Stage four: Meeting in real life. (Perhaps engaging in real sex.)

Why must you wait so long? Because the best relationships are the ones that take time to develop. Not only are you getting to know someone on four different levels, but there are even more ways to woo and be wooed!

Even so, you've probably heard the horror stories about how a match made in cyberspace can be dangerous if you don't take the proper precautions. We're going to tell you about these horror stories again—just in case you've been lulled into believing that bad stuff only happens to other people.

Last year, a thirty-year-old man who was a doctoral candidate at Columbia University in New York (smart, Ivy League, someone your mother might be happy you were dating) tied up, gagged, and sexually tortured a Barnard student he had met and corresponded with on the Internet. He had invited her to his apartment to watch a video. Twenty hours later, the damsel managed to escape and alert the police.

On the flip side, a forty-six-year-old man from New York

City was falsely accused of beating and raping a forty-one-year-old woman from Syracuse, New York, whom he met on the Net. Their first encounter was in a chat room, which led to a six-week exchange of E-mails. They decided to have a real-life date in New York, where the man invited her to his apartment for a home-cooked meal. Wrong!

After dinner, the two had sex, and, the next day, the woman left a message on his answering machine saying how much she enjoyed the evening. He called her back, saying that he, too, had a good time, but he didn't think that the relationship had a future. The creepette proceeded to call the police and accuse the man of raping and beating her. He was led away in handcuffs and his picture (and business home page) were splashed across the papers and TV news broadcasts.

Now that you're scared out of your mind, let's put it all in perspective. Tales like these make the newspapers because the Internet as dating service is still new enough to pique people's interest. The bar scene and personal ads have all done their time going through the media mill as fodder for murder mysteries and thrillers. (Remember *Looking for Mr. Goodbar* and *Sea of Love*?)

The fact is, date rape is a serious social problem that can happen anywhere, anytime, in anytown, to anyone. Even when the guy comes from a good family (does the William Kennedy Smith trial ring any bells?), or is famous (Mike Tyson), or is a friend of a friend of a friend. You just never know. We are *not* blaming the victim here, but both the Barnard student and the man who was falsely accused of rape made the same near-fatal mistake—they met their cyberdates in an apartment instead of a public place!

Yes, there are some rules and regs when it comes to finding love on-line. As in real life, there are plenty of wolves who use the Net to lurk around for us chickens (no offense to the endangered animals, which we think are quite lovely). Here's how to play it safe and keep the cyberwolves at bay when trolling the Net:

1. Remember that the guys you meet on-line are strangers. You may *think* you know him inside and outside after all you've shared with each other. You don't. Dating in real life is the best way to get to know someone. If the guy is pressuring you for sex (he shouldn't), keep the relationship on-line until you feel comfortable taking it to the next step.

2. Don't believe everything you read. Glen may really be Glenda and JohnEAngel may really be LucIfer.

3. Don't respond to lewd or crude messages. There are a lot of pubescent pests in cyberspace who get off on flaming (sending obscene messages to) others. It is best to ignore them. If you're in a chat room that has a host, let him or her play bouncer. You can click the "ignore" button on any offender's name in your room list box. After that, all of the "troll's" chat remarks will be hidden. Change your screen name if the messages continue.

4. Report obscene E-mails to the cybercops. You can exterminate the pests on AOL by forwarding the obscene message to the Terms of Service (TOS) department at: TOSEMail1, TOSEMail2, or TOSEmail3.

5. Meet in a public place. Unless and until you've done all your research about someone you've met on-line, have your first date in a public place such as a café, bar, or restaurant (see our list of cybercafés on pp. 179–187). Meet on your turf, where you feel in control of your surroundings. Lunches or coffee meetings are better than dinners for first dates. They're shorter and, if you're not clicking or you're feeling uncomfortable, you can always say, "Sorry, gotta go back to work."

6. Don't give out your phone number, Social Security number, credit card number, or password. Get *his* phone number, if you're interested. Even if you've met the guy in real life, wait until you're absolutely certain that he's safe before you give him your phone number. You call him instead. And when you do, hit *67 to disable Caller ID.

Never, ever reveal your password, even if the person says he works for your on-line service. A real employee would never request your password. If someone tells you there's a problem with your service and he needs your credit card number in order to sign you up again, ask for his full name and telephone number, and say you have to call him back. Immediately contact your service provider.

7. Don't use your E-mail address at work to date. Not only is dating at work distracting, but you could also unwittingly supply your boss or colleagues with some juicy reading material. Some companies consider their E-mail system company property, which means Big Brother might be watching, as well as reading your E-mail.

8. Trust your gut. Instincts, that is. If your on-line partner seems insincere, strange, or weird, stop corresponding. Change your screen name if you have to.

9. Don't type anything that you wouldn't want read over a loudspeaker. People have very little control over where their words go once they've been launched into cyberspace. Your messages could land in just about anyone's inbox, so be careful.

10. Have realistic expectations. Like any form of dating, there are no guarantees that the man you've fallen in love with on-line will ask for your hand in real life. Keep your desperation in check and look at cyberdating as another romantic adventure.

11. Don't believe everything you read. Anybody, and we mean anybody, can publish something on the Net. Seeing something in print does not necessarily mean it's true.

If you are assaulted by someone you met on-line, call the police immediately, and ask your Internet provider to keep a record of the messages that you exchanged with the man who attacked you. There are computer crime experts who will seize the perpetrator's computer as evidence.

Here's how one safety-savvy cyberdater handled an uncomfortable situation. "I made a date to have brunch in New York with a guy I met from an on-line personal ad," recalls Abby, a thirty-three-year-old marketing director from Manhattan. "Our plan was to meet right outside the restaurant. He drove up alongside the restaurant where I was standing, stuck his head out the window, and invited me to get into the car while he looked for a parking spot. I said, 'That's okay, I'll wait right here for you.' He seemed startled by that, but there was no way I was getting into the car with a total stranger." Way to go, Abby!

So what should I do when my cyberbeau says he's ready to talk to me in a real life?

Congratulations, you are entering the second stage of your relationship—the telephone. At this point, no matter how excited you might be about getting to the second stage, say, "That would be great. Give me your phone number and I'll call you."

Never, never give a guy your phone number until you've done your research. Until you feel comfortable that he is the genuine article (i.e., not married, perverted, or in jail), you should be the one to make the calls. Here's an example of an exchange that one woman nipped in the bud because of insufficient information:

> Rock95: Any garter belts in your lingerie drawer?
>
> SheMD: Who are you?
>
> Rock95: An interested party.
>
> SheMD: I'm not in a room, how did you find me?

Rock95: I have my ways.

SheMD: Must know.

Rock95: I asked first.

SheMD: Do I know you?

Rock95: Maybe. Answer the question.

SheMD: Not till you tell me how you know me.

Rock95: I just found you, I don't know you.

SheMD: How did you find me? This is my business screen name.

Rock95: I'll tell you how I found you once you answer.

Rock95: Hello?

SheMD: Waiting for you to answer about your system for finding people. Gotta know.

Rock95: Not until I get my answer.

This is when SheMD wisely logged off. Don't fool around with someone who may turn out to be a stalker or worse. If the guy continues to invade your screen, report him to your on-line service guide. If it doesn't stop, call the police. They have special computer crime units and can work with your phone company and server to weed out the offending party.

Even if you never give out your phone number, you may come across a guy who has Caller ID. This allows the person you're calling to see your phone number before he picks up. This happened to Tracy, a thirty-eight-year-old teacher from Wisconsin. Wisely, she hadn't given out her number, but she called a guy who had given her his number in an E-mail message. She left this message on his answering machine: "Hi, this is your computer pal Tracy. Sorry I missed you. I'll try again tomorrow." Five minutes later her phone rang. He had Caller ID.

You can press *67 before you make any call in order to block Caller ID from being used by the person you're calling. Having to do this each time could be a pain if you are planning to call a lot of guys you don't know. In that case, you should contact your local phone company about getting an "All Call Restrict" Caller ID disabler. Unfortunately, the service is not guaranteed to work 100 percent of the time, and it does not work on long-distance calls. But it's free, so why not use it while taking other precautions as well.

Phone Books On-Line

Going live? AOL now has an on-line version of the national white and yellow pages. You can even search a directory of AT&T toll-free numbers. All you have to do is go to Keyword: Phonebook. Just click the directory you want to use, type in the name you're looking for, and the appropriate city. Then, click "search." If the number is listed, you'll have it in seconds. But beware: If you can do this, so can your cyberpals. So keep your last name close to your vest, or tell the phone company not to give out your number.

Phone Books on Line (Cont.)

If you want to search for someone's E-mail address, try www.four11.com, which works just like the telephone information service 411. Plug in the name and city of the person you're looking for and it will slog through the 10 million white-page listings for that person's E-mail address. Bigfoot (www.bigfoot.com) works the same way, and www.switchboard.com also does searches for business E-mail addresses.

When should I call him? I usually like to let the guy make the first move, but I don't want to give out my phone number.

You're smart not to give out your phone number so fast. But that does put you in the position of having to call him first, which we understand is uncomfortable for many women. If he lives in the same town, and you are sure that he is safe to meet in person, set up a date via E-mail following the safety net rules we've addressed in this chapter. Then, if you are interested in seeing him again, give him your phone number.

Baudy Books

It had to happen. Novels about on-line romances are popping up in bookstores everywhere. Two that we've heard about are *As Francesca* by Martha Baer (Broadway Books) and *Chat* by Nan McCarthy (Peachpit Press). *As Francesca* is the story of a woman named Elaine who crunches numbers by day and keyboards by night. Single and alone in her apartment, Elaine transforms herself into "Francesca," the willing sexual slave to her cyberlover "Inez." One passage from the novel by Baer, the executive editor of *Hotwired,* goes like this.

> " 'Get . . . down,' " Elaine remembers Inez saying. "And there'd be a moment, right about then, when I'd start to hear my own breathing. I was indecent. I was incorrigible. . . . And then, long breaths later, the letters would spill across the screen. They'd come quickly like fingers executing a musical scale. 'Get down on your knees and shut your mouth.' "

One reviewer for *The New York Times* called *As Francesca* ". . . neither alluring nor effective." (A bit of a slap, which means that Elaine might have enjoyed it.)

Chat, an epistolary novel about an E-mail love affair, has gotten some positive on-line buzz. McCarthy, a tech writer with marketing savvy, launched a Web site to promote the novel, and says she gets more than 500 hits a day from *Chat* fans wanting to talk to the author or to the main characters in the book. The success of *Chat* has prompted McCarthy to write two sequels, *Crash* and *Connect.* You can visit her site at http://www.rainwater.com.

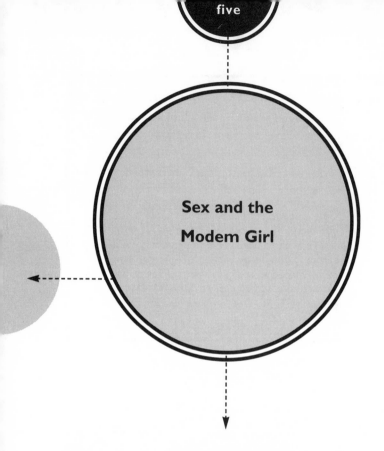

five

Sex and the Modem Girl

A GUIDE TO CYBERSEX

Not since the advent of the VCR has technology so profoundly changed our sex lives. Before the VCR, porno flicks were seen by frat boys and men in raincoats in some skeevy red-light district cinema. Now both men and women can go to their neighborhood video store and rent *Betty Bops Boston* to watch in the privacy of their own bedrooms.

The same goes for cybersex. Not so long ago, men who wanted to engage in some fantasy sex would dial 900-BIG-BUTT with the telephone meter running every breathless minute. Today, interactive, virtual sex is available to anyone who wants to boot up some booty. Whatever your fantasy or fetish, you can find it on the Net.

Cybersex is certainly fun, but it has created myriad social and moral issues, some of which we deal with in this chapter and some of which we tackle in Chapter 7, The Tangled Web. We hope that the following Q&As will help guide you through your cybersexual adventures—whether you're squeezing into your naughty miniskirt as LustyGrrl or batting your electronic lashes as TrustyGrrl.

Should I ever invite a man into a private room?

A private room can be many things, depending on what you're looking for. It can be the virtual equivalent to stepping outside for some fresh air at a crowded party, or renting a hotel room for a romantic tryst. The answer to your question, however, is you might not have to. On-line gender ratios being what they are, a woman entering a chat room will be immediately swarmed by suitors, many of whom will beg you to chat (or have cybersex) with them in a private room. It all depends on your level of comfort at making the first move.

If you see someone who interests you (by his scintillating conversation or profile), you can always suggest a private rendezvous by sending him a private message. Select a room name that only the two of you will know about (private rooms do not appear on the member room list) and click in. This way, if he rejects your advances (unlikely, but it could happen), you won't be humiliated in front of the entire chat room.

Of course, a cybernymph can and will do whatever she wants. If it's cybersex you're craving, you will find more than enough horny men eager for your invitation. But let us state again for the record: In the on-line world, a woman never has to make the first move if she doesn't want to. How nice to be worshiped!

Should I "go to bed" on the first date?

That depends on what you want to get out of the encounter. Always keep in mind that the cyberworld is very similar to the real world. It's possible to meet a guy at a bar who you're really attracted to, sleep with him that night, and end up with a serious relationship and, possibly, a wedding ring. But the chances of that happening are slim. As in real life, love at first site is the stuff of fairy tales and movies.

By "going to bed" with a guy you just met on-line, he might think that you have cybersex with *every* guy you meet on-line. That doesn't mean there aren't plenty of reasons why you might want to have an innocent fling at the keyboard. If you are between boyfriends and you haven't had real sex in a long time, cybersex can be the next best thing to being there.

The first thing you need to do is choose a sexy screen name. That way your "good girl" persona can keep her moral standards intact, while the cyberslut does whatever the heck she pleases (or pleases her). Cybersex is perfectly safe (viruses can't be spread from computer to human), and it's fun to let the wild side of your personality get her yayas out without practicing what you type in real life. Remember, unless you reveal your real name or other screen names, no one will know it's you who is "sleeping around."

I've met someone who I've been having great cybersex and phone sex with for months. I'd like to try it in real life. Should I go for it?

To be safe, arrange to meet in a public place for a drink, coffee, or lunch first. (See the preceding chapter, The Safety Net.) You should also let a friend know where you are going and give her the guy's phone number and E-mail address. Make sure you call her when you return from the date to let her know you're all right (and to give her details on the date).

If you've done your research and you are 100 percent sure that this guy has no rap sheet, you can take the plunge. Of course, there is also the risk of being disappointed by what you see in person. That's why it's important not to misrepresent yourself with someone whom you would like to meet in real life. (See also Chapter 7, The Tangled Web.)

I want to try cybersex, but I'm not used to talking dirty. Any suggestions?

Guys *love* to talk dirty. Guys also love it when women talk dirty. (Why do you think 900 lines are so popular?) Thanks to the Net, men can explore their wildest fantasies without taking out their credit card, and women can write the things they might not feel comfortable actually saying to their partner in bed.

Typing dirty can open up a whole new side to your sexuality, *especially* if you're the kind of woman who blushes at the word "penis." Once you master the fine art of typing dirty, you might find yourself being more adventurous in bed. We know many women whose sex lives have improved after practicing their sexy prose on some lucky recipient.

Like any good sexual experience, there should be an equal give and take when having cybersex. Since some men tend to finish quickly, we suggest letting him pleasure you first before you take care of his needs. The women we've interviewed who have had frequent cybersex say men tend to be much more attentive in cyberspace than they are in real life.

So take advantage of his generosity by letting him seduce you (e.g., "I'm kissing your breasts. :* :* :* Now I'm sucking on your nipples."), while you sit back, relax, and enjoy the show. If you need some ideas about what men want women to say or do to them, read a few *Penthouse* letters, or watch an X-rated video.

Pretend to *be* that woman in the centerfold or porn flick. (Hey, look at all the money you'll save on implants.) Most women (if they're honest about it) have faked an orgasm or two. Just fake it on the screen.

Dirty Typing

We thought you might enjoy a sampling of cybersex between a photographer and a female TV reporter from a large metropolis who decided to consummate their relationship in a private room. :::sweating:::

CyJon: Welcome JenE . . . What are you wearing tonight?

JenE: Blouse and panties.

CyJon: I'm in faded jeans and a crisp, white Armani shirt. You smell terrific . . . Come on over and sit on the love seat with me.

JenE: I'm walking over . . .

CyJon: And quite a walk it is!

JenE: I'm snuggling up . . . I'm leaning my head against your chest and throwing my legs over the end of the love seat.

CyJon: Our lips touch . . . Your soft, sweet tongue parts my lips . . . mmmm . . . I kiss you deeply . . . I loooove kissing . . . (a lost art).

JenE: I bite, no nibble, your lip just a bit so you know I'm serious.

CyJon: Mmmm . . . mischievous lil' JenE. You open the buttons of my shirt and feel the heat of my body . . .

JenE: You're aching for me . . .

Dirty Typing (Cont.)

CyJon: I lift up your blouse ... Tell me about your breasts ...

JenE: Much more than a handful ... round, firm ... my nipples are hard. We press together, sink into each other ...

CyJon: I love feeling your body against me ... I gently move my finger around the circle of your breast ... seeing your taut nipples excites me ...

JenE: And me ...

CyJon: I take your nipple between my thumb and forefinger and gently roll back and forth ... TOUCH YOURSELF, JenE, FEEL ME THERE ...

JenE: I feel you ...

CyJon: Now my hungry mouth replaces my hands ...

JenE: Bury your face into my breasts.

CyJon: Mmmm ... you are delicious ... I feel your nipples rise to meet my hot tongue ...

JenE: You hear me moan ... I want you to keep going.

CyJon: My hand finds your hot mound under your lacy panties . . . I press down and move in slow circles . . .

JenE: I throw my head back and let out a sexy purrrr . . .

CyJon: I slowly lower your panties . . . you lift up your sweet ass to help . . . You are already so hot and wet . . .

JenE: I quiver in anticipation . . . and I am!

CyJon: I'm kissing your soft, inner thigh.

JenE: Hmmmm . . . I could faint with pleasure . . .

CyJon: I open up my belt buckle and undo my snap . . . wanna help?

JenE: I pull your shirttails up out of your pants . . . I kiss your stomach.

CyJon: Mmmm, your mouth is so hot.

JenE: Unzipping, you burst out . . .

CyJon: See what you do to me?

JenE: Little kisses . . . licks . . .

CyJon: Oh Goddd . . .

JenE: I slowly take you in my mouth.

CyJon: Take me deep, JenE.

JenE: My hand surrounds you and grips just so.

> **Dirty Typing (Cont.)**
>
> CyJon: I love watching my thick cock sliding be-
> tween your full, sexy lips. My cock is
> growing inside your mouth.
>
> JenE: You feel my tongue all around you. Our
> rhythm is in sync.
>
> CyJon: I'M ALMOST THERE...I'M GONNA
> CUMMM.
>
> JenE: Give me...
>
> CyJon: YOU'RE THE BEST. MARRY ME!!!
>
> JenE: Half grin.

Will great cybersex lead to great real-life sex?

Meeting someone who you've had sex with on-line can be scary. There's no guarantee that you will be attracted to each other in real life, even if the cybersex was steamy. You're going to be much more reserved face-to-face. But you will probably know quickly if there's a second date in your future.

Your chances of meeting the man of your dreams on-line are a little better than meeting a guy in a bar, especially if your attraction to one another is based on more than just sex.

One friend, who had great cybersex with a guy she met on-line, had real-life sex that was just as hot and wonderful. The reason the sex was so good, she said, is that they both knew exactly what the other one wanted in bed.

Another adventurous cybercouple who wanted to maintain their anonymity decided to meet at a designated hotel. Since they had never actually seen one another in person, they wanted to maintain their anonymity (a big turn-on for both of them) by meeting blindfolded in the room. They kept the lights off and had sex without ever removing their blindfolds. They eventually took off their blindfolds as well as their clothes.

Of course, we wouldn't recommend doing this with someone who you haven't thoroughly checked out first. (See Chapter 4, The Safety Net.)

Guys are always asking me what I'm wearing when I'm on-line. Should I put on something sexy to get myself in the mood?

The great thing about computer dating is that you don't have to wear makeup or a miniskirt to attract a man. If certain things help get you in the mood, fine. You might try playing your favorite romantic music in the background or lighting some candles.

If you meet a guy in the Dungeon, which is a chat room for lovers of S&M on AOL, then you will want to mention the black leather teddy and spiked heels that are pressing against his naked flesh, even if you're swaddled in sweatpants. Most guys love anything out of the Victoria's Secret catalog or

Frederick's of Hollywood. Remember, the mind is a powerful sex organ. As with reading a sexy novel, your imagination is the best aphrodisiac.

What are some fun ways to enjoy cybersex?

Cybersex can also be used to spice up an existing relationship. One way to do this is to have your boyfriend watch you have cybersex with another man. A lot of guys find this kind of voyeurism a huge turn-on, and this is a safe and completely anonymous way to invite a third party into your bedroom. You don't have to tell the guy you're having cybersex with that there is someone else in the room. Or, if you want a ménage à trois, find another adventurous man or woman on-line who wants to join you in some wild fun.

If you're too shy to invite another actual person onto your screen, you can always create an imaginary third partner. You can take turns describing what he or she is doing with you in bed.

It might also be interesting for you or your boyfriend to switch screen names and to sign on as each other. You can enter a sex-oriented room and see what it's like being the opposite sex on-line. One of our male friends did this, and was amazed by the feeling of power he got from being the object of desire. He signed off before he actually had cybersex with anyone, but said he had a lot of fun flirting as a woman.

You can also have cybersex with each other as completely different people. One night you can be a blonde showgirl with 42DDs who meets her dates at a seedy cocktail lounge in Vegas, and the next night you can be a slender, dark-eyed, raven-haired flight attendant with small, perky breasts, who lures a passenger into joining the Mile High Club. It's your fantasy— let yourself go. The most powerful sex organ of all is between your ears, not between your legs.

Cybersexus Interruptus (A Transcript)

The following proves that, as in real life, not all cybersex sessions are created equal. We don't know where this fictional tidbit originated, but we suspect that the boys from Wall Street or Silicon Valley had something to do with its appearance on the Net.

Wellhung: Hello, sweetheart. What do you look like?

Sweetheart: I'm wearing a red silk blouse, miniskirt, and high heels. I work out every day. I'm toned and perfect. My measurements are 36-24-36. What do you look like?

Wellhung: I'm 6'3" and about 200 pounds. I wear glasses and I have on a pair of blue sweatpants I just bought at Wal-Mart. I'm also wearing a T-shirt with a few spots of barbecue sauce on it from dinner . . . It smells funny.

Sweetheart: I want you. Would you like to screw me?

Cybersexus Interruptus (A Transcript) (Cont.)

Wellhung: OK.

Sweetheart: We're in my bedroom. I'm looking up into your eyes, smiling. My hand works its way down to your crotch and begins to fondle your huge, swelling bulge.

Wellhung: I'm taking hold of your blouse and sliding it off slowly.

Sweetheart: I'm throwing my head back in pleasure. The cool silk slides off my warm skin.

Wellhung: My hand suddenly jerks spastically and accidently rips a hole in your blouse. I'm sorry.

Sweetheart: That's OK. It wasn't really too expensive.

Wellhung: I'll pay for it.

Sweetheart: Don't worry about it. I'm wearing a lacy black bra. My soft breasts are rising and falling as I breathe harder and harder.

Wellhung: I'm fumbling with the clasp on your bra. I think it's stuck. Do you have any scissors?

Sweetheart: I'm reaching back, undoing the clasp. The bra slides off my body. The air caresses my breasts.

Wellhung: How did you do that? I'm picking up the bra and inspecting it.

Sweetheart: I'm arching my back. Oh baby.

Wellhung: I'm dropping the bra. Now I'm licking your, you know, breasts. They're neat!

Sweetheart: I'm running my fingers through your hair. Now I'm nibbling your ear.

Wellhung: I suddenly sneeze. Your breasts are covered with spit and phlegm.

Sweetheart: What?!

Wellhung: I'm so sorry. Really.

Sweetheart: That's OK. I'm pulling your sweat-pants down and rubbing your hard tool.

Wellhung: I'm screaming like a woman. Your hands are cold! Yeeee!

Sweetheart: I'm pulling up my miniskirt. Take off my panties.

Wellhung: I'm pulling off your panties. My tongue is going all over, in and out, nibbling on your . . . umm . . . wait a minute . . . I've got a pubic hair caught in my throat. I'm choking.

Cybersexus Interruptus (A Transcript) (Cont.)

Sweetheart: Are you OK?

Wellhung: I'm having a coughing fit. I'm turning all red.

Sweetheart: Can I get you a glass of water?

Wellhung: No, thanks. I'm fine.

Sweetheart: I'm tuggin' off your pants. I'm moaning. I want you so badly.

Wellhung: Me, too.

Sweetheart: Your pants are off. I kiss you passionately—our naked bodies pressing together.

Wellhung: Your face is pushing my glasses into my face. It hurts.

Sweetheart: Why don't you take off your glasses?

Wellhung: OK, but I can't see very well without them. I place my glasses on the night table.

Sweetheart: I'm bending over the bed. Give it to me, baby!

Wellhung: I have to pee. I'm fumbling my way blindly across the room and toward the bathroom.

Sweetheart: Hurry back, lover.

Wellhung: I find the bathroom and it's dark. I'm feeling around for the toilet. I lift the lid.

> Sweetheart: I'm waiting eagerly for your return.
>
> Wellhung: I'm done going. I'm feeling around for the flush handle, but I can't find it. Uh-oh!
>
> Sweetheart: What's the matter now?
>
> Wellhung: I've realized that I've peed into your laundry hamper by mistake. Sorry, again.
>
> Sweetheart: Mmm.

Is cybersex ever better than the real thing?

We think there's nothing like the real thing. That being said, any sex is better than no sex. Cybersex can be great if you have a side to your sexuality that you wouldn't feel comfortable exploring in real life.

For guys, there is no anxiety about performance because he's only as big, hard, and good as he writes. For women, you don't have to worry about how you look taking off your panty hose. What you do during or after cybersex, of course, is up to you. You might get really good at typing with one hand.

Remember to keep your other screen names and personalities a secret. If the guy you're cyberdating, but not very serious about, knows you also go under MstrsX, he can locate you in a room having cybersex with another man. Have one name professionally, one for meeting guys, and one for friends. Keep the different parts of your personalities separate. You can always change your screen name for variety or safety's sake.

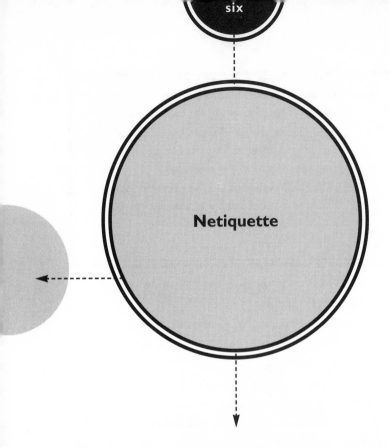

six

Netiquette

Although it may seem a bit like the Wild West out there on the Net—there *are* codes of behavior that govern each and every one of us who goes on-line. For some, the anonymity of cyberspace makes it tempting to verbally shoot people down like a disgruntled postal worker. But keep in mind that there are on-line service sheriffs who will lock you out of cyberspace if you break the rules. As in real life, always be polite, law-abiding, and please don't litter.

What's the best way to end a conversation on-line?

Since a great deal of intimate on-line socializing happens in the wee hours of the night, "I've got to get up early tomorrow," seems to work well for many people. If it's only 8:30 P.M., the simple and vague, "I've got to go," will suffice. It's none of his business what you're doing after you sign off.

Be careful about going into another chat room if you've made up some lame excuse. Lisa was caught having a conversation with another guy after she left a cybersuitor. He sent her an instant message saying, "Hey, I thought you were going to bed!"

This doesn't mean that you stay on-line with some guy forever out of politeness. Think of it this way: would you talk to the same guy at a party all night without circulating? Being inaccessible at first can help pique a man's interest.

If you don't want to continue your conversation with a guy, you can simply say, "Gotta go" or "BFN" (bye for now). If you plan to sign on again, use another screen name. Whatever exit line you choose, be polite. Even on-line, you have to be careful of men's egos.

What's the best way to make a chat-room entrance?

There's nothing worse than going to a party where you know absolutely no one. People are talking in little cliques that seem like impenetrable gates of steel to the outsider. This is what it's like to be the newbie kid on the block trying to enter a chat room. If you trip by asking some foolish question (Jodie's biggest fear), and tumble head over heels in front of the cackling group, no one will respect you and—even worse—no one will answer what you thought was a cleverly worded question.

Fortunately, the Internet is filled with files, help areas, and men who are willing to take you by the hand and guide you through the initial social awkwardness. Be friendly, open-minded, and a good listener. Say "Hi" to the room when you enter, and lurk for a while until you can pick up the jargon and get the gist of what's going on.

If you find certain things confusing, click into the FAQs box, which contains the most "Frequently Asked Questions" about that group or room. First impressions do mean something.

When Things Go Haywire

Here's an example of what can happen when feelings get hurt in a chat room. This letter was sent by an insulted person to the offender and "cc'ed" to a dozen others. (Screen names have all been changed to protect the guilty and innocent.)

Dear Laura,

I was told that you were talking about me when I wasn't on-line. It is not illegal to log a room. It is a function under "file" that anyone can use. Many of you are not aware that AOL logs everything on-line, including IMs and E-mail. That is how many sex offenders have been caught.

Keep in mind that I have logs of your typing a depiction of a gun aimed at my screen name—another thing that happened when I was *not* on-line. Also, I have the room log where Caryn5 says she will make up things to get SueMe thrown off of AOL by circulating a petition. I have copies of two death threats from FreeHold. Death threats are a federal crime, not just an AOL crime.

I don't care if you continue your games in the chat room. I think you should know that most of your real names are public information on the Internet. I don't think your bosses would be pleased to know that their employees are playing around on-line during work hours. I don't think your spouses would like to know what some of you are doing on-line. (It's laughable the way TouchE manipulates many of you to feed his libido.)

The sad thing is that you are ruining the room for decent singles out there. Most of you should think before you type.

How do I join a newsgroup that's been around for a while?

No one likes an ill-mannered person, on- or off-line. There are several rules of thumb when joining a newsgroup:

• With the exception of sex, if you wouldn't do it in real life, don't do it on the Net. Be polite and ask questions (after you've checked out the FAQs on the newsgroup) in a non-threatening way. Don't start flame wars (an exchange of nasty messages) just because you disagree with something someone has said. If you wouldn't call someone you disagreed with an asshole to his face, don't call him an asshole on the screen.

• Watch your spelling. There is no greater universal turn-off in the Networld than a miserable speller. Although a bad speller is not always an idiot, it's like bad posture—it gives the appearance of a sloppy mind. Also, don't use big words to show off your smarts. It's pedantic, er, we mean, pompous.

• DON'T USE ALL CAPS. There's no reason to shout out your messages. It's loud, rude, and uncivilized.

• When you've read a post you agree with, don't copy the entire post to the group, adding, "Well said!" or "Ditto!" You're wasting valuable space by not bringing anything to the party, and people tend to get irritable when they see such waste.

• Do not respond to trolls who post offensive messages just to get a rise out of someone. Responding to trolls, no matter how brilliant the retort, is exactly what they want you to do.

• When you reply to a message, remind the recipient of the original message by quoting some key sentences.

• Keep your emoticons in check. An occasional grin, $<g>$, is fine to indicate irony or a joke, but go easy on the smileys.

I'm over 40 and single. Should I lie about my age?

If you feel uncomfortable about revealing your age, you can try what Patty did. For the line in her member profile asking for her birth date, she chose Gemini, preferring to leave Net surfers guessing about her age. She had just turned forty, and was a bit worried that her on-line suitors would pass her by for a younger woman. As it turned out, there was no need for concern. "If the guys turn out to be younger, I usually get a comment from them about how sexy the idea of an older woman is to them," Patty says. "Some guys will always start out by asking your age."

If it's a long-term relationship you want, it's best to be honest. If it's a night of cyberpassion, then be whatever age you want to be. Your computer can be a virtual fountain of youth.

How should I break up with a guy I met on-line? Can I do it by E-mail, or is that cowardly?

It depends on how far your relationship has progressed. If you've met in real life, you definitely owe him a phone call. But if you've only dated on-line, an on-line kiss-off (meaning a virtual kiss :* good-bye) is fine. Maura, a thirty-year-old flight attendant from Chicago, remembers being dumped via E-mail by one guy she had been dating in real life. Very cold.

Let's take it from worst way to best way. The worst way to break up with a virtual partner is to disappear into cyberspace by changing your screen name. This should be reserved for escaping stalkers, spam (junk E-mail), or flames only.

The next most cowardly way to break up is by not responding to IMs, E-mails, or other attempts at communication. Put yourself in the dumpee's shoes. Remember you're dealing with a living, breathing, human being on the other end of the wires. No one likes to be ignored to death.

The best way to break up with someone on-line is to deal with them directly and as honestly as possible. You may want to break up because you've met someone else on-line, or because you're jealous that he's been going on too many virtual dates. Or perhaps you feel the relationship has no real potential. Whatever. All are legitimate reasons to take flight. But do so like the mature, new millennium woman that you are.

If I'm not interested in a guy who responds to my personal ad (I've gotten so many), do I say, "No, thank you," or just ignore his message?

The best way to provoke the ire of a man's feelings on-line is by not responding to his E-mail. In fact, it's the number-one complaint we've heard from men about on-line dating. Lisa discovered this the hard way after placing her ad in Match.com. Like you, she got so many responses that she didn't have time to get back to each and every guy who E-mailed her.

As a result, Lisa got a number of sulky messages from jilted suitors, including this one: "Why haven't you responded to my message? Is it the picture? I took a lot of time to write to you, the least you could do is acknowledge that you received my E-mail."

Even when she did respond, albeit hastily, to one man who had written her, she was equally chastened: "You never met me, never heard my voice. Your interpretation of my letter says more about you than about me. I regret having written you."

Moral: Always remember that feelings do get hurt, on-line and off-line. If someone takes the time to write you their whole life story, a well-thought-out response (even if it's a rejection) is in order. If the guy rips off a one-liner such as, "Love to hear from you," you can either ignore the message or respond in kind.

A courtesy response to those men you are interested in is the polite thing to do. Say something like, "Thanks so much for your message. I got a lot of responses to my ad and I'd like to get back to everyone, so please be patient. I will be in touch soon."

If you're not interested in meeting the guy, for whatever reason, let him down gently so you don't keep him hanging. (You wouldn't want to be!) Never say you didn't like his picture, line of work, or description. Say instead, "Thanks so much for responding to my ad. Based on your message (and my own quirky needs), I don't think we are a perfect match. But thanks, again, for writing and good luck in your search!" If he just sent a picture, you might want to say, "Thanks for sending your photo. You look nice, but I'm attracted to a different type."

If you've had a few E-mail exchanges with a guy but they fell flat, you can say, "It was really nice talking to you, but I don't really think the chemistry is there for a romance. Good luck in your search." For men, and many women, bad news is often better than no news at all.

Elbows Off the Computer Table

When Emily Post first penned her now-classic etiquette guide in 1922, her concerns were mostly about engraved invitations, proper introductions, and how to eat finger food without embarrassing yourself and your family. Two generations later, her successor, Peggy Post, has discarded the pen for the computer and added a section on "electronic communication" in her seventy-fifth anniversary edition.

In addition to warning people against being "reckless and rude" in their E-mail or chat conversations, Post includes the following "Ten Commandments for Computer Ethics," produced by the Computer Ethics Institute (did you even know there was one?).

1. Thou shalt not use a computer to harm other people.
2. Thou shalt not interfere with other people's computer work.
3. Thou shalt not snoop around in other people's files.
4. Thou shalt not use a computer to steal.
5. Thou shalt not use a computer to bear false witness.
6. Thou shalt not use or copy software for which you have not paid.

7. Thou shalt not use other people's computer resources without authorization.
8. Thou shalt not appropriate other people's intellectual output.
9. Thou shalt think about the social consequences of the program you write.
10. Thou shalt use a computer in ways that show consideration and respect.

Sometimes I'm too tired when I come home from work to answer my E-mail. Am I being rude by not responding?

In a way. The great thing about E-mail is that it's fast, so you don't have to wait for the postman to ring twice. The polite thing to do is to answer your E-mail by the end of the day, if only to acknowledge that you received it. If you're too tired to respond at length, just say, "Got your message. Long day at work. I'll E-mail you tomorrow."

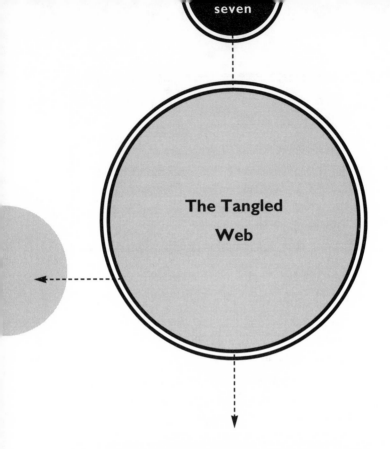

seven

The Tangled Web

LYING, CHEATING, AND OTHER DECEPTIONS

A lot has been written about the how cyberdating has become fertile ground for the unscrupulous. Sure, there are liars and adulterers in cyberspace. But creeps are everywhere—including in your neighborhood bar, nightclub, or sports stadium. The trick is knowing how to separate the good guys from the bad.

At the risk of seeming paranoid, Netgirls need to watch out for themselves in the same way women have to be careful when walking alone down an unfamiliar street. You don't have to clutch your purse to your chest, but a little caution and skepticism is advised.

How do I spot a married man?

Unfortunately, the cyberworld is crawling with married men looking for what they believe is a little innocent, extra-marital fun. In cyberspace, there is no tan line on the ring finger or physical clues to check to see if he's lying. You could start by looking at his member profile, although married men who are interested in cybersex probably won't admit to being hitched.

You can also ask him point-blank: "I get the feeling that you're married. Are you? If so, I must tell you that I'm not interested in taking this conversation any further." Sometimes a direct question will evoke a truthful answer. Or, if he signs off shortly afterward, you also have your answer.

Married to the Modem

Here are some red flags that the man you're cyberdating might be married.

- He never wants to give you his home phone number.
- He only wants to talk to you during the day when he's at work.

> **Married to the Modem (Cont.)**
> - He's chatting with you while he's at home, but suddenly has to sign off. (Chances are his wife just walked into the room.)
> - Your relationship is purely cybersexual.
> - He offers to meet you face-to-face far away from where he lives.

If I have cybersex with a married man, is that cheating?

People tend to be split on the issue of whether cybersex with someone other than one's spouse is cheating. Some men we've interviewed seem to be in favor of the practice as long as *they* are the ones who are doing the cyberflinging. The sex-obsessed shock jock Howard Stern (famous for his real-life fidelity to wife Alison) readily admits to spending hours in his basement jerking off to the words of lonely women. He says it's innocent fun that prevents him from cheating on his wife in real life.

George Topp, a married writer for *Esquire* said his cyberfling with a woman he meet on-line actually improved his marital sex life by producing some fodder for his fantasies. "Ultimately, [cybersex] seems to me to be no worse than, oh, staring at a Cowboys cheerleader," Topp wrote. However, he later added that "if it were my real-life wife doing a virtual lapdance on somebody else's laptop, I'd be more than *virtually* pissed." Why the double standard, George?

We believe you need to follow your own moral compass about this. However, if your ultimate goal is a serious relationship, it's in your best interest to assiduously avoid married men on-line *and* off-line.

Liaisons Dangereuses

Not everyone agrees about what constitutes infidelity when married folk go on-line. The following real-life examples of extramarital cyberrelationships illustrate how some E-mails can lead to *liaisons dangereuse*.

Last year, a New Jersey man filed for divorce after discovering his wife's sexually explicit E-mails to another man who called himself The Weasel. The husband, John Goydan, claimed that he was computer-cuckolded by his wife, Diane, who exchanged erotic fantasies and cyberkisses, even though she never actually met The Weasel in real life. Goydan is suing for custody of their two children, and Diane is claiming that her husband defamed her and that his search of her E-mail was a breach of privacy.

In another case, Howard Eskin, a TV sportscaster and self-described king of in-your-face talk radio in Philadelphia, sent a dozen real roses to Marlene Stumpf, forty-seven, whom he had met on-line, prompting her husband to stab her to death in a jealous rage.

Eskin said he had written Stumpf six long E-mail messages, responding to what he had sensed was a marriage in

Liaisons Dangereuses (Cont.)

trouble. The forty-five-year-old Eskin, who is married with four kids, admitted that he had consoled Stumpf through his E-mail notes and that about four weeks after their first virtual meeting, he sent her some real flowers. "All I was trying to do was brighten up her day," Eskin told the *Philadelphia Inquirer.*

Lest you accuse Eskin of being a lothario who in some indirect way triggered Marlene's untimely demise, according to another article in the *Philadelphia Daily News,* Stumpf apparently had five or six other cyberrelationships, at least one of which she consummated in real life.

If you've already fallen, you're probably not going to listen to our advice, but here it is anyway: Walk away now. Unless he's willing to leave his wife for you, the only relationship you can expect from him is cyberlove or mistress. If you haven't hit the sheets yet, it's not too late to turn back. Promise us you'll start surfing immediately for another more appropriate love interest, which means someone who doesn't have ring around the finger.

I think my cyberbeau is cheating on me with another cybergal. Is there a way to tell if he's strayed?

Welcome to high-tech torture. Although computers have provided us with a new way to meet single men, they've also have given us a whole new way to cheat. If you're on AOL, you can find out where your lothario is by using the following lethal feature in the digital dating game.

Go to the Members window, drag down to "locate a member," and enter the guy's name in the open box. A message will pop up telling you if he's on-line, and where. If you discover that he is in a "private room," it's like catching your boyfriend checking into a hotel with another woman. You can comfort yourself, however, by knowing that he is at home with at least one hand on the keyboard.

If you are really going out of your mind with jealousy and anguish, you can try one Net-savvy girl's trick of the trade: the cybersting. Change your screen name and try seducing him in your new persona. Janet tried this with a guy she had met on-line. She signed on using another name, found him on-line, and entered the chat room that he was in. She flirted shamelessly with him, sent him a private message, and soon he was uttering the familiar phrases and little jokes that she once thought were for her eyes only.

What did she do with this information? Nothing. She decided not to confront him, since, she had to admit, it was a devious way to check his fidelity. But at least she now knew what she could expect from him in real life.

I lied about my looks on-line. How can I ever meet him in person?

Never use your Playmate persona with guys you intend to become serious with unless you really look like one. It's okay for a bit of meaningless (but delicious) sex, but you are setting yourself up for a fall if you've completely misrepresented yourself.

That doesn't mean you shouldn't emphasize your best physical qualities when asked the inevitable: "What do you look like?" If you have heavy thighs, talk about your beautiful hair, eyes, or face. It's not lying, it's just good editing. We know this is difficult for many women who are conditioned to look at themselves in the mirror and see only the negative. Hopefully, by the time you meet a guy in person, he will have fallen in love with the *inside* you, regardless of what's on the outside.

That's what happened to Jim and Carol, one couple who'd had frequent cybersex after meeting on-line but not in person. After months of long-distance Internetcourse (Jim lives in Atlanta and Carol is from Seattle), Jim wanted to meet face-to-face. He made plane reservations for Carol three times and, all three times, she had some excuse about why she couldn't come. She got the flu. Work obligations. Whatever.

Eventually, Jim decided he would surprise her by flying to Washington. After touching down, he called her from the airport. She had to tell him the reason she was afraid to see him. It seems she was not the Kate Moss–like waif she had portrayed herself to be on-line. In truth, she was overweight.

Instead of taking the red-eye back to Atlanta, Jim insisted on seeing her. Yes, she was overweight. He couldn't care less. They had a great weekend together and they are still in touch by phone and Net. In fact, their only problem is the 3,000-mile chasm between them.

The moral of this story? It is possible for someone to fall in love with who you are inside. That's why cyberlove is especially good for women with what society deems "average" looks and bodies. You know what they say in high school—people who might not be knockouts often develop a better personality or intellect than that cute cheerleader or hunky football player.

For them, the Internet can be the empty canvas on which they paint a stunning self-portrait. This was the case for one wheelchair-bound woman who met her future husband on-line. Would she have felt comfortable rolling over toes in a singles bar? Probably not. But she managed to find a man who fell in love with the woman inside her less-than-perfect body. That's what we call true love.

How can I tell if a guy is lying, just to get me to rip off my virtual clothes?

Most of the time you can't. When you're talking to a guy in person, you've got physical clues to help you determine if a guy is on the up-and-up. If he doesn't make eye contact, for example, smiles inappropriately, or shifts nervously in his chair, something's not kosher.

When you're on-line, however, it's often difficult to tell the difference between boldface type and a boldface lie. There are, however, certain tricks to catching a guy in a

Web of lies. If he says he's from your hometown, and you don't think he is, talk about some landmark, store, or restaurant that only locals would know about. If he pretends to love reading the classics, ask him about his favorite books and authors. In time, the liar will usually slip up and, if he's lying about these "little" things, he may be just as untrustworthy about bigger issues.

The most common things men lie about are their height, length, and income. Women lie, too, of course, mostly about their age and weight. These little fibs (or big lies depending on the size of the exaggeration) are often forgiven when the relationship progresses and the prevaricator finally comes clean.

The scam artist, on the other hand, lies for fun as well as profit. These guys can spin a total fantasy life, stringing the unsuspecting woman along by pushing all the right emotional hot buttons. If you're not careful, you could get roped into a cybersex relationship that's emotionally draining or headed nowhere.

The scam artist might also try to bilk you of some hard-earned cash by giving you some cock-and-bull story about how he needs a temporary loan to start that new business that he *knows* is going to bring you the financial rewards you deserve. Never give money or credit card numbers to anyone, no matter how nice and honest he seems or how long you've been E-mailing each other.

What are some of the red flags to watch out for with guys I'm chatting with on-line?

Trust your instincts. If there is something in what a guy is saying or the way he's saying it that doesn't sit right (remember, you don't have the physical cues to go by in cyberspace), ask him to clarify. If you don't like his answer, move on. A good way to spot a red flag is if you find yourself asking your girlfriends to help you decipher your conversations (e.g., "Bob said I remind him of his mother. What do you think that means?").

Also, if there are long, long pauses between private messages, it could mean that he's chatting with someone else while he's talking to you.

I'm having so much fun going on-line as SexySadie that I never log on as myself anymore. My real personality is too boring.

You're never going to meet a guy on-line or off-line if you can't accept or be your real self. Changing personalities is something that we can do for fun, or for a little cybersex, but it's not a great way to start a serious relationship. The fact is, SexySadie is a part of the real you; you just have to learn how to incorporate her into your other personality. Once you do, you might find that you're not as boring as you think you are.

How do I know if I'm having cybersex with a sixteen-year-old computer dweeb?

Cybersex with a sixteen-year-old computer dweeb is harmless if you're also a sixteen-year-old computer dweeb. But if you're over eighteen and you're consorting with a minor, you could be dangerously close to breaking the law. In one recent case, a forty-year-old man was having a cyberrelationship with a twelve-year-old girl who was fooled into thinking he was seventeen years old. The sicko somehow convinced the girl to send him a video of herself in compromising positions. He was eventually arrested.

Fortunately, most women do not go looking for love in the playgrounds. You'll probably know that your cyberbeau is a young one by his less-than-mature sexual techniques. (Although it can be difficult to tell sometimes, since men often revert back to that hormonally volcanic period in their lives.) Nevertheless, teenage boys usually don't possess the verbal skills of a man with more mileage than stamina under his belt.

You can try making references to events that occurred before his birth. If he thinks Watergate is a kinky-sex Web site, you might have a little Beavis or Butthead on your screen. Threaten to tell his mother on him. If that fails, threaten to report him to your computer service guide, the on-line equivalent of the principal. The naughty boy may get his computer privileges suspended.

I met this guy on the Net two months ago. He thinks I'm an erotic dancer, but I'm really a legal secretary. Now he wants to meet face-to-face. What do I do?

Come clean before you meet. He might be lying about his profession, too. Plus, it might not matter to him if your conversations were more than just verbal lapdancing. If you hit it off, go on a date to an upscale topless bar and explore the fantasy in real life.

How do I spot a gender bender?

There's no real way to tell for sure if you're chatting with a man or a woman. It's always a good idea, though, to check the profile of the person you're chatting with. He or she might have been too lazy to change it or make up a new one. But MIT psychologist Sherry Turkle, author of *The Second Self: Computers and the Human Spirit,* says that more men than women go on-line as the opposite sex, so it's more of problem for men looking for women than the other way around.

"An interesting thing happens with men when they log on as women," Turkle told *Working Woman* magazine. "One thing they often come across is how irritating the harassment is. That wasn't what they had in mind when they logged on as women."

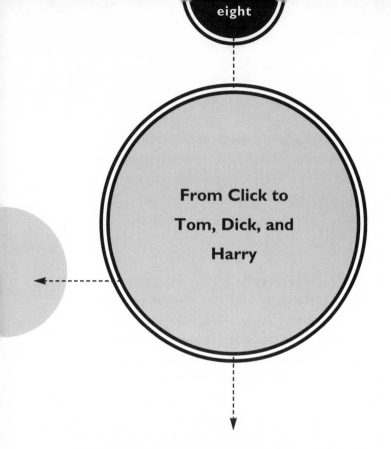

eight

From Click to
Tom, Dick, and
Harry

**TIPS ON PLACING AND ANSWERING PERSONAL ADS
ON-LINE**

On-line personals are the same as placing a personal ad in a magazine, only faster and cheaper. In fact, many on-line personals are practically free. Where most magazines charge per word or character, you pay no more than your service-connection time. So go easy on the acronyms and be as descriptive and specific as possible. This is advertising, girlfriends, so we're talking demographics, target marketing, and giving good copy.

How do I place or answer an on-line personal ad?

Here's how. Be specific about yourself and about what you're looking for in a partner. For example: "SBF seeks real-life love" says almost nothing. "Sexy, 5'6", 125-pound, 30-year-old, SF of Jamaican descent seeks intelligent, hard-working, hard-bodied man of color from So. California. My law practice has kept me from dating, but I'm ready now to take a romantic plunge. Must be interested in a serious relationship . . . " says volumes more.

You can be witty, but don't be too mysterious or over the top. You'll attract too many freaks that way. We've found the ads that get the most attention are a combination of witty *and* revealing. Also, personal ads are not the place to recreate yourself. Be honest. If you're overweight, call yourself "a woman of size," "BBW" (big, beautiful woman), or possessing a "cushy tushy." Some men like to live large.

There are also specialized Web sites, such as Match.com, which charge a nominal monthly fee for browsing the service on an ongoing basis (see Chapter 12, Ladies, Start Your Search Engines). For free personals, check the romance area on your service provider. Choose ads grouped by region, age, or interest.

Once you've chosen, say, Northeast Singles, you can select a specific folder such as Professionals, NYC Suburbs, or Divorced Moms that further narrows your search. Each folder may contain fifty or more ads to read. Pick one or more that attracts you, compose a private response, and send it to the E-mail address. Don't use the "post" button or your reply will be visible to everyone (particularly embarrassing if you are writing the same reply to several ads).

"My first foray into the personals gave me an idea of the types of ads I'd find to help me write my own," Lisa recalls. "But I saw an ad posted that I liked, and I mailed in my response right away. I was attracted to Macky, who described himself as a playwright and poet. Within five minutes of my reply, Macky sent me an instant message. He was on-line when he got my message, he liked what he read, and he came to look for me. We chatted on-line that night, and I took his phone number. Within days we made a date for coffee. Although we never got past the first date, I still use the personals forum to meet and date new men. It's exciting to come home to a inbox full of messages from potential suitors!"

If you're advertising on a national BBS (Bulletin Board Service) or in a newsgroup, put your location in the "subject line." This will save guys from having to read your entire ad before finding out that you live on another continent. And if you see an ad you like, save it, because you never know if it will still be there when you sign on next. Also, if your ad isn't getting the kind of response you'd like, change it.

How do I write an ad that will get a response from the type of guy I'm looking for?

Guys are attracted to ads that seem to speak to them directly and communicate something about who you are. Be specific about what you are looking for in a partner and include as much information as possible about your hobbies and interests. And put yourself in their shoes—men probably aren't as concerned with your profession as they are with your personal life.

What kind of sports do you enjoy watching or participating in? What do you look like? (Compare yourself to a famous person or movie star or a cross between two people so they get a visual image. Don't lie or exaggerate, however.) Where do you live? What are your favorite movies, TV shows, singers, or books? Most important, write it from the heart. Sincere ads will get sincere responses.

How do I reply to an ad that will get him to respond to me?

Tell him why his ad was special to you. The biggest turn-off is the generic response like, "Loved your ad. Check out my profile" or "I'm just your type. Write me." Take the time to respond fully and directly to something that he wrote in his ad. You don't have to write a completely new response each time, but tailor at least the first paragraph to the ad you're responding to, and cut and paste the rest.

I'm afraid to answer a personal ad because I hate being rejected.

So you answered an ad and the guy never responds. How do you get over the rejection? You say, "It's his loss," and you move on. You also remind yourself, "If he didn't want me, why in God's name would I want *him?*" Or take the following advice of sales people, for whom rejection is an occupational hazard: "If you're not getting rejected every day, you're not trying hard enough." Or, as the Japanese proverb goes: "Fall seven times, stand up eight." Also, it gives us some insight into what men must feel like when we reject them. A little sensitivity training isn't bad for the soul. (Refer to Chapter 6, Netiquette.)

I got fifty responses to my personal ad! How do I keep track of all these guys?

Ah, what a nice problem to have. The benefit of chatting on-line is that you can save all your conversations on hard copy and/or disk. Not only is this helpful in keeping all these guys straight (review your conversations before you actually meet them face-to-face), but you can try to pinpoint the trouble spot if something goes haywire in your relationship. In this way, it's a little like the black box in the cockpit of an airplane.

We are not encouraging your neurotic tendency to rehash your emotional distress, but saving and reviewing conversations can be a useful learning tool for avoiding mistakes in the future. And if it all goes well, you've saved your love letters for posterity.

Mostly it creates a record of a guy's vital stats (divorced, kids, age, hobbies, hometown, etc.). There's nothing more annoying than having to go over information that you or he have already given out. And there's nothing more embarrassing than calling someone by the wrong name, or referring to a conversation you had with another suitor.

Although some guys keep files on the women they meet on-line, many find it unnerving. So don't mention you've got a dossier of information on your date that would make the FBI jealous.

Dear Diary

We told you that once you start romancing the Net you will have more suitors than you know what to do with. Well, for those of you who have tried it, we weren't kidding, were we? That's why you might want to keep a record of all the men you're cyberdating along with their profiles so you don't slip and call them by the wrong name.

Not only will this help you keep everyone straight, but it's fun to write down your impressions and experiences as you go along. Of course, you can always pull a Nixon and destroy the incriminating or embarrassing parts once you get hitched.

Dear Diary (Cont.)

You can follow this format or make up your own.

Real name:	Children/names/ages:
Screen name:	Siblings/names:
E-mail address:	His description:
Snail mail address:	Your description of him:
Home phone:	Attach photo/GIF if
Work phone:	applicable:
Hometown:	Impressions (chats, E-mail):
Age/birthday:	Impressions (phone):
Occupation:	Impressions (face-to-face):
Hobbies/interests:	Conversations (include
Single/divorced/	dates):
widowed:	Level of interest:

Help! I was responding to a guy's personal ad that I liked, but clicked "send all" by mistake. Now every guy who E-mailed me is going to think I'm interested in him. What do I do?

Whoops. The guys you mass E-mailed will be confused at first, but if your answer was tailored to that particular fellow, they will realize later that you sent them the wrong E-mail. That doesn't mean that you should ignore the mistake. If it's too late or you're not able to "unsend" the message, send these guys another quick missive saying, "I might have sent you a message by mistake that was meant for someone else. If so, please ignore it. I'm sorry for the confusion."

If they respond with interest to your message, write them a more personal apology explaining your error. Tell them you appreciate their interest, but have already found a match.

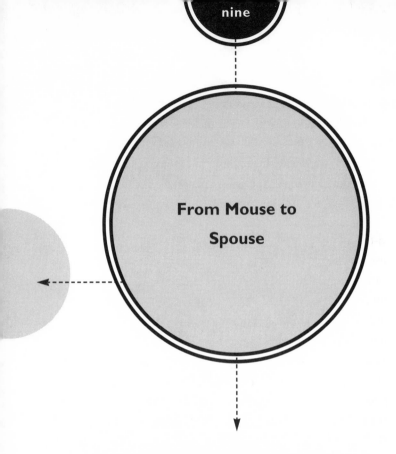

nine

From Mouse to Spouse

REAL-LIFE TALES FROM THE CYBERFRONT

Now that you're armed and ready for your venture into cyberspace, we thought you might want to hear some of the real-life good, bad, and ugly tales from the cyberfront. For inspiration, we've also included success stories. (And there are many!)

Like any voyage, there might be a few bumps and detours

along the way, all of which can be smoothly negotiated as long as you have a sense of humor, a positive attitude, and enough fuel in your emotional tank to continue your journey. Whatever happens, keep hope alive. And have some fun, will ya?

Chevy, 41, Philadelphia, Pennsylvania

"A friend of mine, a beautiful, sweet-natured woman in her mid-thirties, left her husband after years of verbal and physical abuse. She also lost her job and could not afford to pay her attorney or health care for her two children because she wasn't getting any support from her deadbeat ex-husband. She couldn't keep up her mortgage payments and her car was being repossessed. She moved into a tiny apartment with creditors and lawyers chasing her.

"I helped her out as much as I could and tried to be as supportive as possible. One day when she was over at my house, she noticed me playing around with the computer. She said, 'Is it true that people meet each other on-line?' I explained that people meet that way all the time, and I asked her if she wanted me to post a personal ad for her on-line. She didn't own a computer.

"Out of the thirty responses she received, she picked four guys to talk to over the phone. Two dropped out after a few talks and two remained. She met with one guy, whom she didn't like, and another guy who lived two hours away. She kept talking to the second guy, they clicked over the phone, but she was too frightened and battle-weary from her ex-husband to meet him in person.

"After weeks of talking on the phone, the man revealed that he was well-to-do and, without her asking, offered to help her out financially. He asked her for the name of her lawyer and real estate agent, and her creditors' phone numbers.

"Suddenly, all of her credit problems disappeared. He asked her what she did in her previous job, and she said she was a marketing manager. He said, 'Okay, now you're the marketing manager of my company with a salary and health benefits—no strings attached.' She could not put off meeting him any longer. They made a date.

" 'What if you can't stand him?' I asked her. 'I don't care if he looks like a toad,' she said. 'I've fallen in love with him over the phone.'

"The man, whom she had never met before, sent a limousine filled with roses and champagne. She had grown up on a farm and had never been in a limo before. The driver took her to his mansion and they spent a magical weekend together. He took her to plays, shopping, and expensive restaurants. Later, he bought her a car to replace the one that was repossessed and got her a nanny so they could go on a vacation together.

"Needless to say, she fell madly, passionately in love with him, even though he wasn't the type of man she would ordinarily be attracted to. They were engaged after six weeks, and they are now looking for land on which to build an estate (with a large gate to keep her ex-husband out)."

Sarah, 32, Chicago, Illinois

"A while back I was chatting on the IRC, when I met a guy who turned out to live up the street from me. I was living in Israel at the time. Well, we chatted and agreed to meet for dinner. He described himself as extremely gallant, which I like in a man.

"I was starving when I arrived at the designated restaurant. When my sandwich came, the guy quickly snatched half of it off my plate! Then he proceeded to bore the heck out of me for the next hour and a half. After our date, he called me a few times to tell me how much he enjoyed our evening. I said I'd talk to him on the Net sometime, but I never E-mailed him again.

"On the other hand, I've made some great friends via the Internet and I have about four guys I'm in touch with now. If you're savvy, you can weed out the weirdos."

Carole, 49, Stamford, Connecticut

"My story proves that two people who live 3,000 miles apart can meet, fall in love, and marry. Bill was working as a chef in Connecticut. I was working part-time for the DMV and as a substitute teacher in Southern California. I was living with my mother. She had just been told that she had colon cancer and had only a short time to live.

"In November 1991, I signed up with Prodigy. I noticed a post about a video poker game on one of the bulletin boards. Liking the game, I thought I'd respond. It ended up being a six-page note describing how I play the game.

"Bill was one of the numerous people who wrote me back. We started writing back and forth until Christmas, when he left for a two-week vacation with his parents. I had some E-mail waiting for him when he returned home. From that point on, every night we wrote back and forth.

"Then one night Bill gave me his phone number. He suggested that I call him some time. I thought, well, I'm certainly not going to call this man long distance, so I wrote him back, giving him my number. I had barely signed off Prodigy, when the phone started ringing . . . it was Bill. Since Bill was at a loss for words, I was the one who carried most of the conversation.

"By that time, I knew our relationship was something special and Bill felt the same way. We discussed meeting in May, but we soon realized that neither of us wanted to wait that long. I asked for some time off in March, and we decided to meet at McCarron Airport in Las Vegas.

"The night before we were to meet, I dropped a bomb on him. He had told me his age, but I had never told him mine, because I'm fifteen years older. After I told him, he was initially worried about what his family and friends would think. Finally, he said, 'It's my life. I don't care what anyone else thinks.'

"Our planes were due to arrive about ten minutes apart. We had a problem finding each other at the airport, but when we finally did meet, we kissed for the first time. Our trip turned out to be wonderful. Not only did we discover that we were crazy about each other, but we both came home winners. Bill was ahead about $1,000 and I won nearly $3,000. Talk about hitting the jackpot!" (Note: Carole and Bill are now married and the hosts of Prodigy's Personals Connection.)

Jenny, 43, Fullerton, California

"I was a divorced single mom with a young daughter living in Seattle, and Larry was living in the Los Angeles area. After meeting on Match.com, we corresponded via E-mail and telephone for almost a year before we actually got together. We were friends mostly, and since I'd been married before, I wanted to take things slowly.

"I had met some people on Match.com, but no one I really wanted to date more than once. Some of the men were so desperate and needy. In February of last year, Match.com mentioned on their 'zine that they needed volunteers to host real-life parties for members on Valentine's Day. I jumped at the chance because I wanted to meet more people (men and women). In return, Match.com gave me free Venus, Super Search, and Power Browse features.

"The first thing I did when I got my perks was to search the world for men who might become friends or more. I corresponded with about seven men for a while, but they dropped off one by one. I met Larry this way, but even he wrote that he was concerned about the distance when I told him I lived in Seattle. I wrote back, 'What's 1,000 miles between friends?'

"So we become 'puter pals and wrote on a regular basis. The E-mails become longer, and we started talking about relationships and our daughters and our lives. I met someone locally at that time, with whom I had a short but very intense relationship. He got scared and moved on, which hurt me very badly. Larry was there to help me through it.

"Larry suggested that I visit him after Christmas for a few days, as a friend. I had sent him pictures of myself, but when I got off the plane, he told me that the pictures I sent him via E-mail hadn't done me justice and I was more beautiful than he thought. From LAX Airport we went to the Huntington Library and walked through the arboretum and museum area, talking and finding things out about each other.

"He told me at the Huntington Library that he wanted to ask me to marry him, but he thought it was too soon. So he waited until midnight on New Year's Eve to propose. I accepted. I flew back to Seattle on January 3rd with an engagement ring on my hand. We decided to get married on Valentine's Day and, a month later, my daughter and I moved to California. I feel so lucky to have found him."

Richard, 45, San Jose, California

"I'm a divorced, single parent with a sixteen-year-old son. I have never met anyone in a bar. I don't have pickup lines and I don't know what the word cybersex means. I am spiritually oriented (though not religious).

"About a year ago, I started to feel ready to date again. I was nervous about trying too soon because I wanted to be sure not to make the same mistakes I made in the past. Around that time I had just installed a Web browser at work and spent some time surfing the Net every morning. One day I came across Match.com. I had been skeptical about singles services, but decided to give it a try.

"After reading a few profiles, it was obvious to me that people were sincerely looking for relationships, so I posted my own. Over the next year I met about a dozen women, and dated a few of them for a short time.

"Last November I decided to widen my database searches from 30 to 3,000 miles from home. The main reason for this was that I had found two or three E-mail pals who lived far away. I was enjoying the E-mail relationships and thought it would be fun to find a new pal. A few days later Leslie's profile popped up as a 'match.' We began a correspondence. Soon we started expressing interest in becoming more than E-mail pals.

"At first I resisted because she lived on the East Coast. But she persisted, saying that she thought we were soul mates. As a typical male, I resisted this idea, too. After a while I decided to check this out for myself. I closed my office door and went into meditation. As my mind quieted, my heart opened and I got a clear message that Leslie and I were meant to be together.

"Soon we exchanged photos and began talking on the phone. Each step of the process confirmed our intuitions. In December she flew out from New York so we could meet in person. It felt somewhat awkward at first. How often do you meet someone in the flesh that you already know so well in spirit?

"It didn't take long to start to feel comfortable and then, once again, there was the confirmation that what we had was real. She was the *one* I was looking for. She was the one I knew was out there somewhere sleeping under the same moon as I was. What a blessing to have finally come together. She stayed a week. On Valentine's Day I gave her an engagement ring and we plan to marry this summer."

Mary, 24, Milwaukee, Wisconsin

"I didn't like the chat rooms for meeting people. They seemed really tacky. Much of the conversation is cybersex pickups or newbies. Boring! Personals seemed much safer to me, so I put an ad in Match.com and got some good responses. Tom E-mailed me and we had quite a few E-mail conversations before we decided to meet. We exchanged phone numbers and talked, and planned to meet one night for dessert.

"He was into model rockets, and I wanted to learn more about them. I would have just let it go at a brief first meeting and waited to see what developed, but he had a rocket with him and suggested that we put it together if I was interested. That sounded neat, so we went back to my house and built it that evening.

"I would never have invited someone over whom I didn't know, but I had a close friend staying with me for the week, so I felt safe. Plus, Tom just seemed right. I liked his thoughtfulness, so I took a risk. We are now living together and we're extremely happy."

Jennifer, 19, Miami, Florida

"I met my boyfriend in the New Member Lobby on AOL. I had just gotten my computer as a gift and I wanted to see what all the fuss was about. I chatted night and day. After about a month of being on-line, I started talking to a guy who seemed sweet and fun. The problem was, he was eight years older than me and he lived in L.A. while I lived in Miami. We talked on-line more and more, and sent pictures of each other via E-mail.

"I finally said, 'I would love to hear what your voice actually sounds like.' And he said, 'Do you think we should do it? Do you want to talk on the phone?' I remember typing in my phone number and instantly hearing the phone ring. My heart practically stopped. I picked up the phone and heard silence and then a magical voice saying, 'Hello, Jennifer?'

"We ended up with $1,000 in phone bills. I said it would be cheaper for him to fly out to meet me. So he did. We spent a weekend together in Miami. It was perfect. It was strange at first getting used to actually having the person right there with you, but it was so much like when we were on-line or on the phone that we got used to it right away."

Allen, 37, Portland, Oregon

"One night I was hanging out in the Baby Boomer chat room when a woman sent me a private message. She said, 'Are you in the mood for a few bytes?' I said, 'Just a nibble, I'm on a diet.' I guess she read my profile and saw that I was a writer. She works on the business side of a major daily newspaper. We started corresponding every day after that at work and at home.

"Then, she put me on her buddy list. This meant that every time I signed on and she was on-line, she would know (like a reverse Caller ID) where I was. I had no idea what it would be like when I agreed to it. I started getting IMs from her all the time. We stayed in touch and she told me she wanted to get together for brunch. We lingered at the restaurant for a long time and afterward we went for a walk.

"As we talked, I realized that she was just interested in a platonic relationship even though she was writing to me every day. I thought this was weird, and I was sick of the invasion of my privacy, so I asked her to take me off her buddy list. We never spoke again after that.

(Note: Never use the buddy list with someone whom you've just met. Use it for your serious cyberbeau or gal pals only.)

Carla, 30, Phoenix, Arizona

"I started my flight on-line about a year ago with an innocent conversation with a complete stranger from Philadelphia. Chatting is something we are all familiar with in cyberspace, but this was different right from the start. He was in a room that sounded like another off-the-wall sexual deviation to me. So, being sassy, I felt the need to enter and ask a few insincere questions.

"I ended up meeting the most sincere, thoughtful, and intelligent man I've ever had the fortune to meet. A man who had a deep emotional void since being abused as a child. A man with great compassion and insight, who listened intently as I told him about my own abuse story, and how that kind of pain affected me.

"The degree of intimacy we formed through the cyber and optic lines drew our hearts together from what seemed like opposite corners of the world. Late-night on-line chats, E-mail, phone calls, and voice mail. We sent videos and pictures and talked every day. We fell in love. We both sat outside that summer looking at the moon, feeling it was the only way we could look at each other as I stared from Arizona and he from Pennsylvania. We were so far away from each other, yet closer to each other than we had ever been to anyone else in our lives.

"We made plans to meet in real life for the first time. I remember the butterflies as we talked the morning of his flight. 'Gonna be there soon . . . I can't wait to hold you in my arms . . . ' He was so beautiful, standing there. We just smiled at each other. I finally got the courage to touch him and prove to myself that he was truly real. Falling in love is beautiful . . . unless you're both married.

"Although I dream of buying a home in Pennsylvania and teaching my children about how their new father and I met in this strange new universe, I must not. We must not. I must imagine my life without the one who understands me and loves me like no other. I will never forget that day we first touched. I must hide from my children how my heart skips a beat when the phone rings at an unexpected hour. I will not let them see my pain.

"Do I regret that flight that sent me crashing into my lover's arms? I don't know. But I will always cry and feel the bittersweet irony whenever I hear the mention of Philadelphia, that city of (brotherly) love."

(Note: As Carla can attest, on-line relationships between married folk can be extremely intimate even when two people are thousands of miles away from each other and their love is never consummated.)

Ginny, 25, Washington, DC

"Kenny's profile said that he was a military officer, so I E-mailed him to ask what branch of the service he was in. A few days later I got an E-mail from him saying, 'I'm in the Air Force.' I had forgotten who he was, so I had no idea where this message came from! We began corresponding and a few more days passed before I figured it out.

"We soon began talking on the phone and eventually realized that this was God's crazy way of bringing us together. I never thought that this would have happened in a million years. Actually, before this, if someone had told me that she met her husband this way, I would have laughed in her face.

"Kenny and I discovered that we had been in the same exact place at the same exact time (without ever meeting) more than once over the past ten years. Someone or something wanted us to meet this way. I know in my heart that we are soul mates. Here's how he put it in one of his E-mails to me:

" 'I'm very glad that we got to talk to each other. After hanging up, I thought about you all night until I fell asleep. That felt nice, having you on my mind as I drifted off. I, too, feel very close to you, and even though I can't explain why, I don't mind. I'm just glad knowing that somehow we were brought together. That's all that matters to me.

" 'I wish you could be here now, actually. I don't know . . . it's like I've known you for a thousand years, and somehow we got separated. I know that what we have isn't ordinary, and I know we shouldn't let it get away from us.'

"After months of flying back and forth to see each other, he proposed to me on February 14th, and I accepted. Kenny and I will not be in the same state for another six months, but we will be together after that. I wish everyone in the world could understand that meeting someone in cyberspace isn't really as crazy as it seems."

You May :* the Bride

Forget Vegas. When it's time the tie the Net, er, we mean knot with your cyberbeau, why not do it on the very medium that brought you two together? We're talking cyberweddings, kids. Now, GlamOrama's Internet wedding chapel is on-line and available to hitch up the digitally paired. The service includes E-mail invites to your list of cyberguests, all for the low, low cost of $49.95.

Of course, you can always throw your own wedding party by forwarding your own E-mail wedding invites, setting the virtual venue (anywhere your two hearts desire!), and exchanging vows before all of your chat-room pals.

Oh, don't forget to book the judge, pastor, or rabbi. Guaranteed, you will get lots of {{{hugs}}}, smileys ;-), and :* kisses, but no lipstick smudges on your cheeks.

Brian, 49, Hong Kong

"I moved to Hong Kong from London, where I'm originally from. I placed a personal ad on American Singles as a joke. Sometime after, I got an E-mail from Michelle in Oregon, asking me why I was so far away from home.

"It was a fun letter, and I replied. Suddenly we were sending each other E-mails back and forth—up to five a day. Michelle told me about an IRC where we could talk on-line, and our conversations sometimes lasted seven hours at a stretch. We both realized that, in spite of the fact that we thought it not possible, we had fallen in love. Michelle sent me photos and left voice-mail messages for me, but I was too nervous to reciprocate at first.

"When I finally did, we decided to meet in real life and we learned that our feelings for each other were mutual. Soon Michelle is going to find herself a long way from where she was previously living, but very much at home. We are getting married at the end of this month."

Melissa, 30, Ann Arbor, Michigan

"I met my cyberlove last week in real life for the first time. We stayed together for three days and three nights. It was as wonderful as I dreamed it would be. He is even more fabulous in person than he is on-line. We found out we had more in common than we knew, and spent the days and nights doing things that we both enjoyed.

"We both flew to a city that we'd never been to and spent loads of time talking, walking, and sightseeing. We are planning to meet again in a month for a week this time. I can't wait!

"It amazes me that love can really be found on a computer. I know that I don't know everything about him and that I would know him better if we lived in the same place, but I also know that he is a wonderful person and I love him. We felt totally comfortable with each other almost immediately after meeting in real life. I've said over and over that the strangest thing about all of the time we spent together was that it was not at all strange. We felt as though we've known each other for years, not just months on-line and a few days in person.

"To those of you who are about to embark on a similar journey, the only suggestion I can give you is to make sure you have talked to him on the phone first. On-line and phone are different, and the truer personality will come out on the phone, I think. My on-line love and I did not indulge in cybersex either, but we made up for it in person. ::Sigh::"

Rita, 38, Kansas City, Missouri

"I met my partner in the NetNoir chat room. We spoke a lot through IMs and sometimes in the chat room. After a few months, we knew that we liked each other and decided to attempt a relationship. I had plans to visit friends in New York, where he lived, so we arranged to meet each other at the airport.

"He told me what he'd be wearing when he picked me up and gave me a description of himself. He said that he was bald, light-skinned, and that he would be wearing a black leather coat and eyeglasses with dark lenses. I had his GIF for months, so I was sure that I'd recognize him when I saw him.

"Anyway, I walked out of the gate and there was this bald, black man wearing a black leather coat and dark glasses. But he couldn't be Jack, because he was far too dark. So I stood there scanning the crowd and I didn't see any other bald black men in black leather coats. I thought that I'd been left at the airport. That he got tired of waiting for me since my flight was delayed more than hour.

"So there I was about to embarrass myself by crying, when I looked across the room and directly in front of me was a man with a hat on in a black leather coat. I could tell it was him from his eyes. The sun was so bright that day and it was beaming in through the window, so I could actually see his eyes. But I was still not too sure, so I said hello. In my mind I'm laughing now because there was no way that I'd have known it was him because he was wearing a hat. Needless to say, once he opened his mouth I knew it was the right guy—there was no mistaking that voice."

Sharon, 50, Austin, Texas

"The first night I went on the Internet I was browsing through the American Singles profiles for Australia, when I noticed one guy who mentioned that he would be interested in a "lady pen pal from Texas." Being a native of Texas, and noticing that this Aussie seemed to be a nice guy, I decided to E-mail a note to him. He answered it the next day, and we began a strictly 'puter pal relationship knowing that we would probably never have the opportunity to meet face-to-face.

"After many E-mails discussing all the sorts of things that friends easily discuss, we realized that we had a great deal more in common than is usual for two people, especially those who live so far away. We eventually exchanged photos and were both quite pleased with what we saw. Then, one day, he called and we heard each other's voices for the first time. Needless to say, we both thought the other talked funny, but we had become extremely close and felt that we needed to meet in real life or wonder forever about 'the one that got away . . . '

"We had joked many times about having a date on Saturday night. So he made a special effort to come to the United States so we could meet. He arrived on Saturday evening, of course. We discovered that the feelings we had for each other were very real. We were perfectly suited for each other and enjoyed being together so much. The only obstacle was 10,000 miles of Pacific. But that was easily overcome with modern technology <grin>.

"Bill is the best thing that has ever happened to me. He is the man of my dreams and, I believe, my true soul mate. We both know that we would never have met and married if it weren't for cyberspace."

Stephanie, 26, Boston, Massachusetts

"In 1993, I married a man whom I had written E-mail to for months but had only met in person four times. Unfortunately, he lives in Washington, D.C., and I found out the hard way that I can't live in D.C. (the hard way being by trying for a year). I still think the marriage would have survived despite only knowing each other so short a time if it hadn't been for that damned city. We're divorced now, but we're still very good friends.

"Undaunted, I moved to Boston to be with someone else I had met on-line and whom I became involved with. The problem with this relationship was that he only wanted to be involved with someone who lived halfway across the country.

"I subsequently met a guy from Texas, but this time I managed not to move there! He and I had been friends on-line for a long time, and when I was reeling from the loss of the Boston relationship, he was getting over his former on-line girlfriend (who had met someone else on-line).

"In the middle of this relationship (because of the distance between Boston and Dallas, we agreed to see other people), I fooled around with a few guys who I met on-line. One of them had been a friend of mine who I'd talked to for a few years on the MUSH (Multi-User Shared Hallucination). He was coming to Boston, and I offered him a crash space. When he showed up, he was too cute to just leave on the couch, and we wound up sleeping together.

"We've been together two years now. He's moved to Boston to be with me! I'm taking this relationship real slow this time. Advice to other single women on-line: Never make any commitment (which includes 'I love you') to anyone who you haven't met IRL yet. This happens so often and it's just foolish."

Bonnie, 63, St. Louis, Missouri

"I met Bob in the SeniorNet chat room on AOL. Bob had entered the room and did not talk much, and I tried to include him in the conversation. This happened several times. He sent me an IM asking me to meet him in a private room. I had only been in a private room once before and found that things were said that I did not approve of, but I thought that if Bob got out of line I could always leave.

"We went to the private room and talked to each other for more than an hour. We got fairly well acquainted that way.

This happened several times and we exchanged many E-mails. Finally I gave him my phone number and he gave me his. We started talking to each other on the phone. This, of course, allowed us to get even better acquainted.

"He invited me to come to Florida to meet in person and an invitation was extended by his daughter for me to stay with her family while I was there. I met Bob in person and spent two weeks there getting to know him and his family. About six weeks passed and we talked via computer and phone every day.

"He finally came to visit me here in St. Louis and we decided to get married. We drove to Eureka Springs, Arkansas and were married there. Bob has four children and two grand-children; I have one child and three grandchildren. I have met all of Bob's children and I like them all very much. All of our children approve of our marriage."

(Note: It's never too late to find true love.)

Sarah, 26, Seattle, Washington

"When I first met my significant other, he lived in New Hampshire and I lived 3,000 miles away. We had both just signed on to Prodigy. I was haunting the BB called "Vampires," where I could talk to other enthusiasts of vampire mythos. My s.o., Stephen, started posting there, and eventually developed a reputation as a great poet. I was fascinated and started writing to him.

"After that, we started talking on-line and on the phone. He decided finally that he wanted to move here to Washington. Since he was planning to move to San Francisco anyway, it was only a slight detour in his plans. He drove to San Francisco with his roommate (who had also met his new girlfriend on-line), where he stayed for about a month. The day he was driving to Seattle to see me, his car broke down at the California–Oregon border. He called and said that it looked as though we weren't going to get together after all.

"After four months of waiting, I decided he was wrong. At 9:00 P.M., I jumped in my car and took the twelve-hour drive to where his car had broken down so I could pick him up and take him home with me. It's a decision I've never regretted.

Andrea, 21, Boston, Massachusetts

"I've met more than 200 people who I first knew on-line. I'm a frequenter of TinyTim, which has really big parties that attract lots of people. I gave one at my apartment in Boston for about sixty-two people. We have about five or six big parties a year. At New Year's, we had a week-long party in Delaware at the beach that filled two houses. We're a real community that exists both off- and on-line, though on-line is always how we've met first."

Lee, 26, Morristown, New Jersey

"I learned about Jewish Singles through the What's New area of AOL, and decided to check it out. I replied to several ads I saw, and went on a lot of first (and last) dates. I finally double-dated with a woman named Sue. We went to an AOL DJ party, and I left about an hour later.

A few months later, I got tickets to see a band we both liked and invited Sue to go with me. We had talked and E-mailed back and forth since our first date, but that was it. When I invited her to the concert, her first reaction was surprise. She even told me more than once, 'If you meet Ms. Right between now and then, let me know. I'll bow out gracefully.' Well, as it turned out, I had already met Ms. Right!

"We had a great time at the concert, but it was too late for her to go home, so I suggested that she stay over at my place (and I sleep on the couch). She insisted that I sleep in my own bed, so we both did—fully clothed. After the lights went out, I told her to give me her hand. She asked why, and I told her, 'I'm getting a kiss good-night.' I kissed the back of her hand, and we went to sleep. We've been together ever since, and it just keeps getting better! In fact, we're moving in together in a few weeks."

Dawn, 27, Boston, Massachusetts

"It was Christmas 1996, and I was in Philadelphia visiting my parents. I was bored, so I logged onto AOL and went into a singles chat room. At first there weren't many people on-line, but I just hung on and chatted with whoever floated in. All of a sudden, I got an IM from David. I checked out his profile and responded. We had a lot of common interests. My only reservation was that he lived all the way in Florida and I lived in Boston!

"We talked for a long time that night. I didn't expect to hear anything else from him because my other IMs never went anywhere. But we started chatting every night after that in private rooms for at least three or four hours at a time. One night we spent eight hours on-line! It wasn't long before we fell in love, exchanged photos, and sent E-mail and snail mail back and forth. We also shared ideas and dreams of businesses we could start together.

"It felt funny to be in love with someone I never saw in person. But we had so much in common. We laughed at the same things. We had to meet. David was planning to come visit me for Valentine's Day. He said he had a present to give to me. But his plans fell through. He also had a job interview in North Carolina. We entertained the thought of moving there together, but he didn't get the job. David was working as a freelance computer consultant, and money was tight.

"So he took a hard-knock job at a gas station to make some money for a one-way ticket to Boston to visit me. I arranged with a friend to videotape David's arrival in Boston.

I went crazy waiting for his plane to touch down. I have never been so nervous in my life. Finally, we saw each other in person for the first time. We just kept staring at each other and touching a lot. I knew immediately that he was the one."

Beth, 32, Cambridge, Massachusetts

"I have met a man who is kind, caring, sensitive, and educated. In fact, he's a doctor. An M.D. or Ph.D. was my minimum education requirement in my personal ad on American Singles (a bit presumptuous perhaps). I'm a graduate student of chemistry and I really needed to meet someone who could communicate with me on an intellectual level.

"Even with my stringent requirements I had a good number of responses. Although some of the men who responded were a bit strange, most of the men were decent and respectful. I think cyberdating is the only way to meet people these days. My boyfriend and I have been seeing each other for seven weeks. We have a great time together and feel so fortunate to have met. I am certain that we will eventually marry and that we will be together for a long time."

Faith, 42, Sante Fe, New Mexico

"Greg and I started E-mailing each other last year. After a month of long letters every day, we started phone contact. We cherish the hours we spent on the phone, becoming friends, and supporting each other through our respective divorces. Eventually, we fell in love.

"We commute almost every weekend, making the eight-hour drive to be together for one-and-a-half days. But I know that we are in love by the pain I feel when we are not together. Someday soon this nightmare of the distance between us will be over and we will hold each other in our arms always and forever."

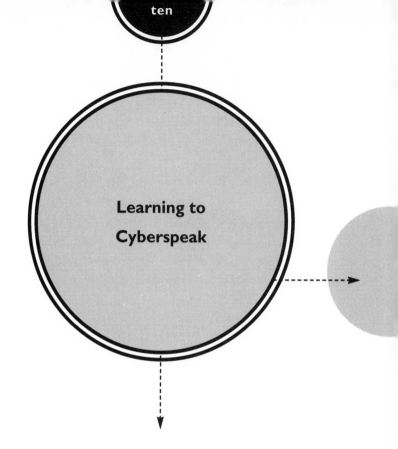

ten

Learning to Cyberspeak

EMOTICONS

And you thought smiley faces went out in the '70s. The Internet has created a whole new graphic language that can be understood by anyone from any country (as long as they cock their head to the left). Some of them are truly creative—a lot of them are downright goofy.

The problem with emoticons is that they take time to draw,

so they will slow you down a bit if you're in the middle of a conversation. At best, they can dress up an otherwise drabby text by adding a touch of visual emotion. Use them if you must, enjoy them if you do.

:)	The common smiley face.
:-)	Variations on the smiley theme.
:-(*or* :(	Sad.
:'(	Crying.
;-)	A wink.
~-)	Another wink.
{}	A hug.
{{{{}}}}	A big hug.
:-I	A noncommittal face.
-->-->--}@	A rose.
12x-->-->--}@	A dozen roses.
:*	A kiss.
:P*	A French kiss.
8-)	A person wearing glasses.
:-0	A look of surprise.
8--0	Oh, no! It's Mr. Bill.
<I:-)	A smile from someone wearing a hat.
:-)~	Drooling.
:-/	Skeptical.
%-6	Brain-dead.
:-D	Laughing.

-:-)	A punk.
:)(:	Two-faced.
#:-)	Bad hair day.
:#	Censored.
:*)	Clowning around.
:W	Whispering.
: x	My lips are sealed.
B-)	Smiling with sunglasses.
:-&	Tongue-tied.
:pPpPpPpP	Giving somebody a raspberry.
:-J	Tongue-in-cheek comment.
<:)))><	A fish.
3:-o	A cow.
.V	A duck.
8:]	A gorilla.
}:>	Devil.
O:)	Angel.
====:}	A snake.
∧=======∧	Burning the candle at both ends.
*∧5	High five.
Y	A wine glass.
<G>	Grin.
<BG>	Big grin.
#$@%*	Expletive.
. . . --- . . .	SOS.
::poof::	Outa here (signing off).

::waving::	Hi, everybody (signing on).
(((-!-)))	Mooning or shaking your booty.
\(!)/	Virtual intercourse.

ON-LINE SHORTHAND

Since time is of the essence when you're looking for love, Netfolk want to cut directly to the chase by using shorthand, or acronyms, to say as much as they can in the least space possible. Here are some common phrases that we've seen on the Net. Use them sparingly, or else your messages could end up looking like a jumble of alphabyte soup.

AFAIK	As far as I know.
AFK	Away from keyboard.
ASAP	As soon as possible.
B&D	Bondage and discipline.
BBL	Be back later.
BBS	Bulletin Board System.
BBW	Big, beautiful women.
BTW	By the way.
BRB	Be right back.
C U L8r	See you later.
D&S	Dominance and submission.
DIKY	Do I know you?
DILLIGAF	Does it look like I give a fuck?
F2F	Face-to-face.

FAQs	Frequently asked questions.
FOAF	Friend of a friend.
FTA	Fun/travel/adventure (used in personal ads).
FUBR	Fucked-up beyond repair.
FYA	For your amusement.
FYI	For your information.
FWIW	For what it's worth.
GA	Go ahead. Keep talking.
GAL	Get a life!
G/B	Gay/bisexual.
GF	Girlfriend.
GIF	Graphics Interchange Format (used to send photos).
GMTA	Great minds think alike.
HNG	Horny Net geek (stay away from them).
HOUEW	Hanging on your every word.
ILY	I love you.
IKWUM	I know what you mean.
IM	Instant Message.
IMHO	In my humble opinion.
IOW	In other words.
IRC	Internet Relay Chat (what happens in a chat room).
IRL	In real life.
IRT	In regard to.
ISO	In search of (used a lot in personal ads).

ISP	Internet Service Provider (AOL, Prodigy, etc.).
ITMT	In the meantime.
JPEG	Joint photography experts group (a picture format).
KMYF	Kiss me you fool.
LAB&TUD	Life's a bitch and then you die.
LDR	Long-distance relationship.
LJBF	Let's just be friends (the kiss-off).
LOL	Laughing out loud.
LTNS	Long time no see.
LTR	Long-term relationship.
NYL	No, you're lying.
OIC	Oh, I see.
OMG	Oh my God!
OTOH	On the other hand.
NAC	Naked at computer.
NFW	No fucking way!
PDA	Public display of affection.
PITA	Pain in the ass.
POV	Point of view.
ReHI	Hi again (used in chat rooms).
RI	Romantic intent.
RT	Real time.
ROTFL	Rolling on the floor laughing.
RTFM	Read the fucking manual.
S/A C	Sex, age check.

S&M Sadism and masochism.

SNAFU Situation normal—all fucked-up.

SNAG Sensitive New Age guy.

SO Significant other.

STD Sexually transmitted disease.

STS Skin-to-skin.

SWMBO She who must be obeyed (domme).

HWMBO He who must be obeyed (dom).

TIA Thanks in advance.

TPTB The powers that be.

TTFN Ta-ta for now.

TTYL Talk to you later.

URL Uniform resource locator (Web address).

V/A Verbal abuse.

WWW World Wide Web.

WRT With respect to.

WTG Way to go!

WTGP Want to go private?

WUF Where you from?

YIWGP Yes. I will go private.

YKINMK Your kink is not my kink.

YRS Yeah, right, sure.

GLOSSARY OF CYBERTERMS

Being the tight-knit community that it is (*the whole entire world*), the Internet has its own jargon that should be studied and committed to memory so as not to miss the slightest nuance in communication. The fact is, you'll probably pick most of this stuff up as you go along; you might even end up making up your own words. But it helps to refer to this handy-dandy glossary page when you and your girlfriends are doing a postmortem on the previous night's conversation.

access number The telephone number your modem dials to connect with an Internet Service Provider or Bulletin Board Service.

bash Real-life get-together.

baud The baud rate of a modem is the number of bits it can send or receive per second. The speed of your communication depends on the measured bits per second (BPS).

browser A computer program such as Netscape and Internet Explorer that is used to access information from the Web.

cyber Prefix to anything computer- or web-related. Also short for "cybersex," as in "Want to cyber?"

domain name The individual name that identifies a Web site. Domain names are separated by dots. (For example, http://www.jodiegould.com.)

f Female.

flame Insulting or angry on-line message.

flame war When newsgroup or chat-room participants start flaming each other.

gopher Invented at the University of Minnesota and named for its mascot, this tool directs users to simple, menu-driven lists.

hardwired A feature that cannot be overridden or removed.

keyword A word that automatically accesses information or takes you to a specific area on-line. (For example, Keyword: Romance.)

loft Private room.

m Male.

newbie Someone who is new to on-line communication.

ping A message sent from one computer to another to test if it's active.

punted To lose your modem connection and get zapped from the screen.

search engine A database that contains sites on the Net and their keywords. (For example, Yahoo and Webcrawler.)

spam Messages unrelated to the topic and usually sent to many newsgroups at once.

take a walk Go to a private room.

Telnet A Telnet connection uses remote or host computers, mainly those in university libraries to log on. You can also use Telnet to access your own computer from a remote location.

threads Topic being discussed.

trolls Those annoying, adenoidal boys who get jazzed from shocking on-liners with sexually explicit messages.

Usenet A vast system of newsgroups.

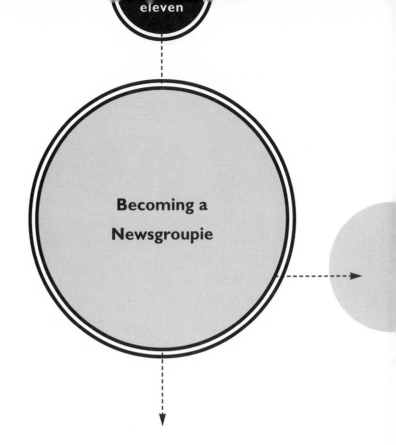

eleven

**Becoming a
Newsgroupie**

A LIST OF NEWSGROUPS AND IRCs

If you can't find one that interests you, start your own. Just follow the guidelines for newsgroup creation in these Usenet FAQs: www.cis.ohio-state.edu/hypertext/faq/usenet; alt.irc; alt.irc.questions; and alt.answers. To view and subscribe to Usenet discussion groups in your area, see www.tilenet.com.

Here are some nonsexual and sex-oriented newsgroups to get you started. (Their subject matters are self-explanatory.)

Nonsexual Newsgroups

news.answers

rec.arts.ascii

alt.backrubs FAQ

alt.beer

bln.humor

alt.humor.best-of-usenet

alt.humor.puns

misc.health.alternative

rec.humor.flame

rec.humor.funny

rec.humor.oracle

news.lists

sci.space.news

alt.sports

alt.tasteless.jokes

Sex and Romance Newsgroups

alt.personals

alt.personals.ads

alt.personals.spanking.punishment

alt.romance FAQ

rec.arts.erotica

alt.sex.exhibitionism

alt.sex.fetish

alt.sex.fetish.fashion

alt.sex.first-time

alt.sex.playboy

alt.sex.stories

alt.sex.telephone

IRC Channels (Dirty Typing)

Although we prefer cybersex with someone we know, at least by screen name, Internet Relay Chats (IRCs) allow you to "speak" to any number of Netfolks looking for some on-line, real-time, down-and-dirty sex talk. We'd be shocked if you met the man of your dreams here, but women have needs, too, and stranger things have happened, so that's why we're telling you about this.

To give you an idea of the size and scope of IRCs, there can be 3,000 participants at any one time, in all time zones, from 150 countries (probably more by now). You can hop from channel to channel, changing your name each time, or you can start your own channels. And, unlike the major services that censor certain topics and language, IRCs are laissez-faire, which is French for anything goes.

Commands on IRCs all start with a slash, like this: /. After you log on, use whatever key or command gets you to an IRC (on some systems, it's simply the command "IRC"). You'll get a series of messages that tell you what software is being used, where the host is located, and how many channels are currently running.

If you're confused, type "/help," and you'll get a list of commands and instructions on how to use them. The number sign: # identifies the name of your channel. To join, all you have to do is type "/join #hottub."

Here are some sex-related IRC channels (we could fill a book with these alone). *Tred safely:*

#bdsm	#passion
#bisex	#polyamor
#bondage	#romance
#crazysex	#romance2
#cybersex	#-sex-
#d&s	#sexy
#dirtysex	#single
#desade	#singles
#Dom/Sub	#spanking
#eroticsex	#sweetsex
#exhibit	#teensex
#kinkysex	#30plus
#lovers	#voyeurs
#loves	#wildsex
#netsex	

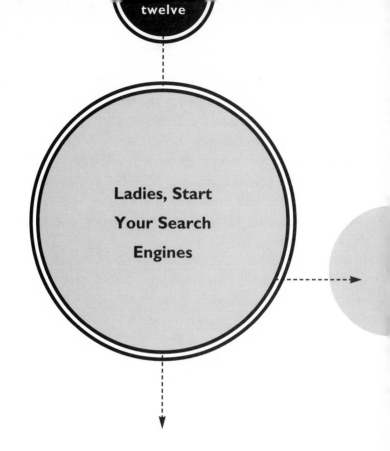

twelve

**Ladies, Start
Your Search
Engines**

**COOL (AND HOT) WEB SITES FOR THE ROMANTICALLY
INCLINED**

It's a wide, wide world on the Internet, but it's definitely worth
exploring. There are hundreds, possibly thousands of Web
sites dedicated to affairs of the heart and other organs. They
can be especially helpful if you want to cast a wider Net in
search of the man of your dreams.

We've selected a few well-known and not-so-well-known Web sites for review, but you can certainly explore on your own with the help of search engines, on-line directories that help locate Web sites by subject. Yahoo, the best and most discriminating search engine around, found 500 sites for our entry "singles." You can access Yahoo (www.yahoo.com), and, from there, jump to the other search engines such as HotBot, Infoseek, and WebCrawler to see what they have for the same keyword.

A few of the others include Alta Vista (www.altavista. digital.com), which found more than 200,000 matches, Lycos (www.lycos.com), which found 20,000 "singles" home pages, and Excite (www.excite.com), which found 93,000. (Bear in mind that some of these finds may refer to singles tennis matches, so you may need to modify your search.) If you want to search the Web from AOL, try www.netfind. aol.com.

Some sites charge for access, but most are free. Assume that all the Web sites listed here are free unless otherwise stated. Many charge a small fee for members, or for services such as sending flowers or kisses. All the addresses start with the prefix http://. (We just didn't feel like typing it in a thousand times.)

Match.com (www.match.com)

With more than 130,000 members and a high profile, thanks to gobs of media attention, Match.com may be the premier site for singles on the Web. They have an inviting and attractively designed home page that you can visit as a member or guest. There is a free ten-day trial period that allows you to test the service before you invest the $9.95 per month subscription fee.

Members can browse the personal ads and photos, searching by age, state, or other criteria. An anonymous handle allows respondents to E-mail you without knowing who you are. Chat areas have different topics, so you can choose your theme and your level of steaminess.

"There are definitely more men on Match.com than women," says one female member from Seattle. "Sometimes the responses can be overwhelming. I have guidelines for IRL dates. My trick is to set a time limit up front. Say you have somewhere to go at 8 P.M., but you can meet for dinner or coffee beforehand. This gives you the opportunity to bow out of the date gracefully."

Mix 'n Match (www.mixnmatch.com/97/04/01/index.html)

Mix 'n Match is an on-line dating-and-mating resource and newsletter for the Match.com Web site. Issues contain a member spotlight featuring a "Couple of the Month" and other success stories, and articles about such things as how to identify four types of guys, and how to get back into the dating game. At "Tell It to Trish," you can get some dating

advice; at "Fools for Love," a Web humorist analyzes foolish behavior.

Talkcity (www.talkcity.com)

This chat Web site features over 300 real-time chats on
subjects from politics, art, hobbies, as well as global problems
and possible solutions. A good place to meet intelligent,
thoughtful surfers.

Cupid's Network (www.cupidnet.com)

Billed as the "world's largest network for singles," Cupid's
Network provides links to tons of events, phone, chat, travel,
and singles sites. This organization casts a wide Net with its
listing of more than 300 singles sites. A great place to start
your search.

American Singles (www.as.org)

American Singles is affiliated with Cupid's Network and
boasts 65,000 members. It provides basic stats for guys whose
full profiles you might want to review. All you get, at first, is
the name, age, and occupation. So if "Jeff, 27, medical student" is enough to catch your fancy, you can look at his listing
for information on his hobbies, interests, and preferences for
a relationship.

Another nifty stat is the number of times Jeff's listing has
been viewed. (If you see 3,495, you might as well click else-

where.) However, women take note: Only 15 percent of the people who use the service are women, which means that women who post their ads here are bound to get a ton of responses. The average age of people who visited this site when we reviewed it was about twenty-three.

Love Plex (www.loveplex.com)

This relationship advice site contains topic areas on "Five Love Personalities," "The Romance Test," "Marital Coma," and the oddly named "A Woman's Brain," which advises guys to help out around the house.

Single Volunteers of America (www.contrex-us.com/sv)

Do good and meet men while you're at it. What more could you want out of an afternoon? This is not a dating service, but offers information on volunteer groups that are sprouting up all over America.

Single Search (www.nsns.com/single-search/)

For those who want to take their search off-line, this site offers a listing of face-to-face, real-life matchmaking services.

Web Personals (www.webpersonals.com)

This is a free service where singles can search personals by keyword and by placing or answering an ad. A "Love Hound" fetches appropriate men and delivers an E-mail to you notifying you of their on-line whereabouts.

TinyTim (www.tim.org)

This link takes you to TinyTim, a MUSH (Multi-User Shared Hallucination) game where hundreds of romances have apparently started between players. MUDs are typically accessed via telnet. Log in as a guest and read the help text.

Singles Online, a Worldwide Community of Singles (www.singlesonline.com)

You've heard of personal trainers? Well, this site offers advice from *personals* trainers, or "relationship coaches" who will speak to you by phone for a fee. You can read their credentials and E-mail them one free question. In the "A Man's Life" area of this site, men can choose "Make Your Wife Like New" or "Become a Sex Object." Not only is the former category not good English, but it smacks of retro-relationship stuff à la "My wife, I think I'll keep her." (This was a '70s TV ad that became a national joke and fodder for the feminist movement.)

Single Sites (www.singlesites.com)

Link up here with national, regional, and religious matchmaking and chat sites for (duh) singles.

Date Central (www.datecentral.com)

This singles connection site offers free access to its computer matchmaking chat rooms, relationship advice, Web site guide, on-line games, astrology charts, and more.

Qpid (www.mainquad.com/qpid.html)

Send a funny greeting card or a valentine all year long. The recipient will get the following message:

> Your gift from Qpid, a shaft of Eros,
> And lasting tribute to Amor.
> But behold! Seven days after sent,
> Gone they are everymore.

Also at this site is "Meeting Street," an on-line service where people can meet one another by searching profiles for similar interests. Membership is free. (By the way, Qpid=cupid, in case you missed it.)

Cyrano Server (www.nando.net/toys/cyrano)

Named for Edmond Rostand's hero who helped a verbally challenged suitor win the woman of his dreams by ghostwriting his love letters, this site will give you ideas about how to compose your prose. You can also read success stories from people so happily in love that they need to shout it from the balcony. Categories include: "Help me dump someone," "Send a valentine," and "Write a love letter for me." Letters are written Mad Libs-style, with the sender supplying the names, adverbs, adjectives, parts of the body. Good for a hoot.

Send a Kiss (www.sendakiss.com.au)

You can send a virtual kiss to anyone with Internet access from this site. We don't quite understand why you can't do this on your own, but hey, this is America, and everything's a product.

Make Me Happy (www.makemehappy.com/)

If flowers make you happy, send a photograph of a flower or bouquet to a loved one (or a friend) through this site. Choose a message from a list of twenty or so including, "Last night was great." And guess what, it's free.

Virtual Flowers (www.virtualflowers.com)

You can pay to send real flowers at this site, or send a free virtual bouquet. But the last time we tried to do this, we got a message saying that the service was "too busy" to handle our request. They apparently send up to 10,000 virtual bouquets per day. That's what we call flower power.

Friends & Lovers (www.cyberspud.com/friends_lovers)

This is a real magazine published out of Florida, so it draws heavily from the printed version, but it's free on the Web.

Place a gratis personal ad, peruse the articles, or chat with someone on staff.

The Love Blender Romance Home Page (www.alienbill.com/romance/)

A bittersweet look at love, where dancing hearts mix it up in a blender. Read sonnets, poems, and readers' thoughts on love.

People Online's Real Love Bytes (www.people.com/sp/love)

Linked to the parent company's Web site on Pathfinder, you'll see a different love issue explored each month, and learn about new books on relationships and intimacy.

Home Arts Kiss Net (www.homearts.com)

Home Arts is the Web site for the Hearst magazine group, publisher of *Cosmopolitan, Redbook, Marie Claire,* and others. From their home page, click on "kiss.net" and from there you can get advice for singles (as well as married folk). Select "talk to others" and then choose by topic. At "The Love Shack," you can read postings from other women about relationships, men's staying power, and ex-girlfriends. There's even a topic on cyberrelationships. This is the homegirl home page. You're not going to meet any guys here.

Car Talk (www.cartalk.com)

"Car Talk," the weekly call-in radio program on National Public Radio, has a Web site that they've been plugging furiously on the air, reports Trixie, thirty-eight, from New York City, our good friend whose sense of humor, style, and playfulness we admire. "The show is witty, and it attracts lots of funny guys," she said. "They have personals on the Web site and, if you post one, you're supposed to describe yourself as a car. I've been writing to this MBA from Columbia who I met here, and we're having an incredibly intense correspondence." Her favorite feature of this site, however, is the "boss button" on the screen, which you can immediately click if your boss walks by while you're playing on the Web during work hours. Up comes a pie chart and other official-looking stuff.

Romance Online (www.romance-online.com)

At this site, you can search members' profiles, or place your own at no charge. But you have to become a member in order to contact someone you're interested in. Fees start at $14.99 per month for unlimited access. Enter the age range and state you're looking for, and up pops a screen full of men. Our request for New York City pulled up only seven men, all in their forties. We'd do better cruising the bookshelves at Barnes & Noble.

Singles Alley (www.singlesalley.com)

James and Carmen are the hosts of Singles Alley, a site designed for singles with "adventurous lifestyles." Does being single in the Big City qualify? This home page promises to "titillate emotions," whatever that means. We checked it out and found nothing very exotic, but maybe trying to meet someone on-line is exotic enough for some people.

The site offers a screen of E-mail addresses with a profile behind each one. The problem is, how do you choose someone by their screen name, or a bunch of letters and numbers? You end up having to look up each one with the chances of their living nearby being slim. But we loved the opening graphics—a dancing logo that caught our eye like babies fixated on a dangling, jangling mobile. Another plus—you can hear each guy in real audio.

Get Met on the Net (www.get-met.com/)

You can register with Get Met by entering a description of yourself and your answers to the following essay questions: How would you describe your perfect partner? Where would your perfect date be and why? What's so special about you? What is the stupidest thing you ever did in a relationship? Frankly, we wouldn't answer these questions on a first date, let alone post them for review by members of the opposite sex.

Safer Sex Page (www.safersex.org/)

This page is loaded with info on safe-sex practices and how to use condoms and other barrier methods. It also contains a Safer Sex forum with ongoing discussions and links to related topics such as STDs, AIDS treatment, women's health, contraception, sex, and sexuality. To borrow the words of home-engineering goddess Martha Stewart, it's a good thing.

Cyber Sex Toys (www.sextoy.com/)

Afraid to walk into your local sex shop to buy a vibrator, dildo, or leather panties? This Web site offers an extensive line of on-line sex-toy products from the fanciful to the fetishistic. The purveyors are careful to warn that "these toys are intended to enhance sexual sensations, not violence." The site also contains parlor games with sexual themes.

Bianca's Smut Shack (www.bianca.com/shack)

For fantasy lovers, Bianca's Smut Shack is an interactive sex-oriented chat room where you can create your own character and identity. If fantasy is your thing, give Bianca a try.

Animal Lovers Personals (www.animalpeople.com)

No, this is not the bestiality Web site. This is for people who have "the greatest pet in the world and the only thing missing is the love of their life." So if you're one of the millions of women with a cat and no boyfriend (Lisa and Jodie are lifelong cat owners), and you're looking for a guy who's not allergic, this is the site for you. Women can place a personal ad for free. And the "Pet of the Month" features a photo of a pet (unclothed) and its owner (fully clothed).

Lisa was tempted to write to a guy who lived three states

away because he listed as one of his strong points "will stop for directions." And when one man listed "Jensen, 8, Allie, 6, and Irving, 5," he was referring to his Siberian huskies, not his kids. Since Jodie met her husband while he was walking his dog Dino, she highly recommends this site and the linking of pet-minded people.

The Love Test (www.topchoice.com/~psyche/lovetest/)

If you love doing those *Cosmo* quizzes and taking tests about love, this is the site for you. The "Concept of Love" test measures what you think about love. The other is the "Experience of Love" test, which measures the amount of love you are experiencing in your current relationship. The tests take about an hour to answer and hosts Betty and Jim will send you back your results and how to interpret the answers.

The Alt Romance Home Page (www.dina.kvl.dk/~fischer/alt.romance/)

Personal home pages of alt.romance people can be found here, and you can also add your own. A link to romance-related resources gives lists of other on-line sites along with advice on dealing with such things as aggressive men on-line. The author, Lars, who is from Denmark and works in the information systems industry, notes that ninety out of one hundred IRCs are filled with men, which is why they pounce on anyone with a female name.

Lars invites readers to stop by his office if they're ever in the neighborhood. (Talk about an open-door policy.) Anyway, Scandinavians seem to know a thing or two about sex and romance, so maybe Lars has some insight after all.

Valentine.com (www.valentine.com)

Look up a lost love, read a literary love letter, or "build a date"—these are a few of the choices at this site. Send a real greeting card for $3.75 by selecting from a collection of romantic, passionate, or flirtatious cards. Pay by credit card and the real post office delivers your hand-addressed missive by snail mail.

The "Love Mechanic" and "Ask Diana" also offer help and advice to the lovelorn. A link to other Web sites takes you deeper and deeper into the love Net. At "Build a Date," you can answer questions about your dream date and then get "matched" with a celebrity who may or may not be married or even the right gender for you. Click on "Best Lines" for readers' suggestions on their favorites. Although, certainly no rival to Shakespeare, we liked:

"Darlin', I'd walk three miles over broken glass in bare feet to kiss the ass of the dog that pissed on the hubcap of the truck that took your panties to the cleaners!"

"Like a wild rose, I want to pick you for myself."

"Your lips are like wine, and tonight I want to get drunk."

"Is this the broom you used to sweep me off my feet?"

"Can I borrow a quarter? I want to call your parents and thank them."

Love at First Site (www.1st-site.com)

To post your profile in this Los Angeles–based site, you must submit a photo and pay a fee of $14 per month. Two typical profiles show photos of guys (where else) at the beach and waterskiing.

WebMatch (www.webmatch.com)

A free on-line personals service with more than 40,000 members. At "Heat of the Week" check out one lucky couple's page. The "Match Me Up" feature automatically E-mails you when a possible match posts his ad. "Love Chat" is available for talking; "Backseat" for advice.

1001 Ways to Be Romantic Page (www.godek.com)

This Web site by author Greg Godek contains excerpts from his five books on romance and relationships, a schedule of his romance seminars across the country, and, you guessed it, 1,001 ways to be romantic. His newsletter of romantic ideas, "The LoveLetter," is also on-line, and you can get a complimentary subscription via snail mail or E-mail. The Web site includes subscribers' real-life love stories and page links to dozens of romance-related sites.

Pulsating hearts greet "computer-industry geeks and normal people" to this site. We really enjoyed the tales from geeks and their most pathetic and embarrassing dating moments. There are also links to articles and other romance sites. Brenda's favorite real personal ads from newspapers are included here, as well as a few on-line personals from her obsession—geeky men.

Gard's Laws on Love (www.scriba.org/~gard/love/laws.html)

A kind of Murphy's Law for daters as written by Gard, a twentysomething Webmaster from Norway (again with the Scandinavians) who is now living in Canada. Gard's Laws include, "If you meet a woman and you like her, she probably has a boyfriend. If she doesn't have a boyfriend, and is interested in you, by the time you realize it, she's not interested in you anymore."

Gard has reprinted a page of more than one hundred ways to say "I love you" in different languages (nineteen ways in Arabic, ten in Japanese, one in Zulu), in case you do get someone to pay attention to you long enough to utter those three, or seven, or two little words. This is more of a site for guys seeking (or geeking) love, but good for some mild amusement and a peek into how the other half grieves, er, we mean lives.

Kiss Me You Fool (www.mindspring.com/community/featurepgs/valentine/)

This site welcomes you with a commercial message for the love product of your choice. Want to express your love? Order Godiva chocolates, cookies, flowers, or perfume. Shopping around with your cyberbeau for an engagement ring? Get diamond advice before you buy. Ask Tracey (everyone's a dating expert!) for dating relationship advice and, once again, link to dozens of other sites dedicated to the pursuit of romance.

The Official Hopeless Romantic's Home Page (www.primenet.com/~ejones/hrhome.html)

Dedicated to providing romance advice to those in need, this site is mostly a collection of articles on gifts to give, pickup lines, poetry, as well as links to other sites on romance. Its "Ring of Romance" includes profiles from Australia and France. Other topics include places to go and things to do on a date for both men and women. To connect with people of color, link up to The African American Home Page with its Singles Connection and Chatpro Realtime One-on-One chat room.

Prodigy Singles Newsletter (www.goodstuff.prodigy.com/lists/singles/)

Prodigy's weekly newsletter for singles is filled with tips, trips, and quips about cyberdating and real-life love (including, egads . . . poetry by members), all edited by a married couple (Carole and Bill) who met in cyberspace and are in this book. The main feature, however, is the male and female Personals and Profiles complete with E-mail address, chat name, age, and thumbnail sketch.

Here's an example from the Female Personals and Profiles:

"Cute, 18, Looking for a sweet someone in FL area who likes candlelit dinners and quiet times. 5'1", 100 lbs, blk hair, brown eyes." You can also browse back issues in the archives at the same address. It will keep you informed about what's happening on Prodigy.

Single Christian Network/SCN (www.singlec.com/)

This site lists men seeking women and vice versa with blurbs about each person, so we don't really know how searchers get a full picture. Respondents are asked to write (not E-mail) a letter to the people they're interested in contacting (using their seven-digit code) and send it to SCN (include $3.00 per letter). Still, it must be working, because a search on Yahoo turned up 21,000 matches made through SCN. Onward Christian lovers!

LoveSearch.com (www.lovesearch.com)

Testimonials, message boards, advice, links, love quizzes . . . it's all here. The Blind Date feature chooses a date for you, given a little information. You could go blind, however, scrolling through all the personal ads.

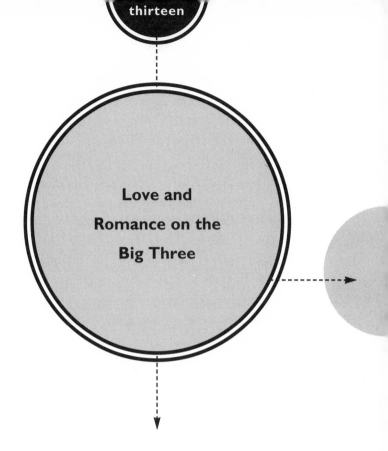

thirteen

**Love and
Romance on the
Big Three**

To access the following romance sites, all you need to do is subscribe to either AOL, CompuServe, or Prodigy. The only difference between these and the previous Web sites is that they cast a smaller Net (i.e., they connect you to fellow members, not the entire World Wide Web).

LOVE AMERICA ONLINE-STYLE

AOL should really stand for Americans Out for Love since it has the largest and most user-friendly romance sites on the Net. If you have AOL, type Keyword: Romance to dial up their Romance Channel and check out the following romantic destinations:

ABC's Love Online (Keywords: abc, love)

ABC's Love Online has teamed up with *Eligible* magazine to offer astrology readings, member bulletin boards, and "advice with attitude" (hey, we thought that was us) from Cyber-Sadie. It's also just a click away from "hotline help," which will answer any questions you might have about AIDS or depression. (Being single can be both dangerous and depressing at times.)

AstroMates (Keyword: Astromates; AstroNet)

Looking for your cosmic soul mate? New Age dudettes can locate guys by keyword, gender, location, or interest. Profiles are placed in categories and there are even pix of some members in the AstroMates gallery.

Digital City (Keyword: Digital City)

Digital City offers picture galleries and personals for big-city gals who want to arrange a date with that urbane, sophisticated man of their dreams. Includes chat and message boards for each major city.

The Gallery (Keyword: Gallery)

This is the place where you can view photographs (GIFs) of your fellow AOL members, or, upload your own lovely visage.

Matchmaker (Keyword: Jewish Singles)

Matchmaker is a personal ads section where your *bashert* (destined one) will be listed under Male Listings by state, or New Male Profiles. Lisa posted a detailed, well-thought-out ad here and was so overwhelmed with responses that she was afraid to turn on her computer! Religious observance (Reform, Conservative, Orthodox) and kosher/nonkosher are all searchable. Message boards also offer topics on issues affecting (who else?) Jewish singles, and two chat rooms entertain singles over and under thirty-five.

Love@aol (Keyword: Love@aol)

One of the most popular romance sites, love@aol is filled with picture personals, dating tips, love letter contests, steamy message boards, and live love chats. Search for your soul mate by common interest, profession, or looks (bronzed, big nose, model, etc.). You can also browse the pix and profiles. The OnQ area is for gay and lesbian personals.

NetGirl (Keyword: NETGIRL)

Look, girls, a site for us! NetGirl is a national bulletin-board dating service with profiles and pix from members all over the country. You can access them by region "Northeast" or "West." There are also chat rooms, CyberLove Polls, a Confession Booth, and a "Dear NetGirl" advice column. NetGirl is available for live, on-line advice from 8:00 P.M. to midnight (EST).

Religion & Beliefs Relationships (Keyword: RB relationships)

This area will help you find a man with a similar religious background. Christianity Online's Marriage Partnership has live chats, messages, and events. And when the time comes, The Knot will help you plan your spiritually enhanced wedding.

Romance Connection (Keyword: Dating or Romance)

This is the granddaddy of AOL's romance areas. The Romance Connection offers personal ads broken down by age, location, astrological sign, and interests. You can use a different screen name here if you want to be anonymous.

Thrive@Healthy Living (Keyword: Thrive)

Obviously, this area focuses on health, fitness, and food. It also deals with sex topics. For these, type Keyword: Thrive@sex.

NetNoir (Keyword: NetNoir)

The self-styled "Soul of Cyberspace," NetNoir (means Black Network) is the voice of Afrocentric culture in cyberspace. Cybergals of color can place a personal ad in "NetNoir Romantics," or post a question that HeartBeat, NetNoir's love coach, can answer. "Romance Noir's Love Chat" is on Mondays at 12:00 P.M. (EST), 9:00 P.M. (PST). You can also visit the Web site at www.netnoir.com. Also check out Keyword: Black Voices for member photos and chat.

Hispanic Online (Keyword: Latino)

This is the Web site for *Hispanic* magazine. It includes a Latino singles chat area: Step into los Chatrooms, Solo En Español, Amistad y Mas (Friendship and More), message boards, and a free newsletter available by subscription.

The Hub (Keyword: Hub)

Cool, flashing, and gyrating graphics greet you at the entrance to this area. Check out LiveGirl's (Lyn Snowden's) message board to see what advice she has on relationship and sex topics, and, for fun, "LiveGirl's Guide to Picking Up Chicks." There's also a topic area on "Questions for the Opposite Sex," where one lassie wanted to know, for example, why men are so obsessed with their old flames. If you actually want to talk to LiveGirl live, dial the Hub on Tuesdays from 12:30 A.M. to 1:30 A.M. (EST). On Thursdays at 12:30 A.M. (EST), Dr. Judy

Kuriansky will answer your sex questions. If you're a Gen Xer, this is probably the site for you.

Passport to Love (Keyword: PPL)

Got a multicultural love? In this AOL site you can read about love customs from other cultures, or send a love letter in Spanish, French, and German. Just fill in the blanks with your loved one's name and a few salient facts, and it's ready to E-mail.

The Bistro (Keyword: Bistro)

Chat rooms are available here in French, Spanish, Italian, German, and Japanese.

PRODIGIES IN LOVE

In addition to the Singles Newsletter, Prodigy has a "Personal Connection" area where members can explore the chat rooms, and a "Singles Bulletin Board" (Jump: Singles BB) where you can post messages (Go/Jump: Prodigy Internet Newsgroup Personal Connection). It also has a male and female personals listing that looks something like this:

E-Mail Address	Chat N.N.	Age	Other
nlkb68@prodigy.com	BigMan	20	Looking for new friends
tgxv96@prodigy.com	Chummy	31	SWM looking for special F

We're told that since Prodigy offered its unlimited $19.95 plan, the chat areas have been hopping. Jump to "chat," then scroll down to "Personal Connections." Here is a partial listing of chat rooms for singles that you'll find on Prodigy Internet or Prodigy Classic.

Age Rooms (Sundays, 10:00 P.M., EST, Ages 35–45ish).
Big Beautiful Women, Big Men Chat (Mondays, 10:00 P.M., EST).
Meet Your Mate Night (Wednesdays, 10:00 P.M., EST).
Singles Pub Room (Mondays and Thursdays, 10:00 P.M., EST).
Single Parents Meet (Check for time).
Disabled Singles (Fridays, 11:00 P.M., EST).
Interracial Dating (Mondays, 11:00 P.M., EST).
Black Singles United (Jump: Damali).

IT'S LOVE/LOVE COMPUSERVE

Who says CompuServe is all business and no pleasure? Okay, so we did, but that's not entirely true. There are about 3,000 special-interest forum areas for people who are looking to meet others with similar passions and interests.

There is a singles message section at the Casual Adult Chat Forum (Go: Chatafor), and at KeyClub Chat Forum (Go: Keychat), you'll find "Get Personal," where you can place and read personal ads. There's also a Private Talk Forum (Go: Talk), for those seeking a private space far from the madding crowd.

When you're in a chat room, you can click on a button to read the screen names of the other people in the room. And, like AOL, you can send and receive private messages (though the sender might very well be from Europe). You can also learn about real-life functions and parties. Three locations that have had shindigs: Las Vegas, Atlanta, and London.

At Who's New On Chat, you can write a sentence or two about yourself, inviting E-mails from trollers. These are not really personal ads, since married folks can post a note about themselves in the interest of simply reaching out to on-line friends, but it's another way to attract the attention of other singles. Here are a few other places you can go for romance.

> **Singles Area (Go: Singles)** You are shown here how to "get connected while connected."
>
> **Singles Schmooze** (Mondays, 10:00 P.M., EST).
>
> **40+ Singles Conference** (Wednesdays, 10:00 P.M., EST).
>
> **World Community Forum** Where you can communicate in other languages.

For other singles-related forums, select "find" from the services list, pull down the menu, and enter the keyword you'd like to search.

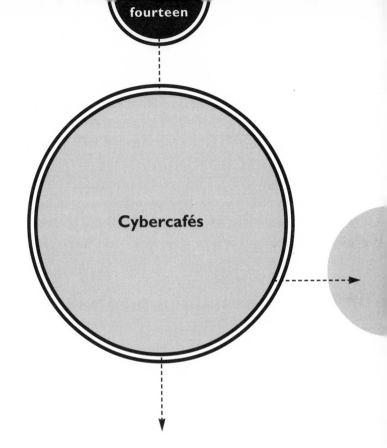

fourteen

Cybercafés

AND OTHER PLACES TO FIND ROMANCE IN THE NEW MILLENNIUM

If we told you once, we told you a zillion times: the whole point of cyberdating is to get your butt off the swivel chair and out into the world. To this end, we are including a list of some popular cybercafés around the country, the meeting place du jour for the computeratti.

We recommend cybercafés for several reasons: In addition to being great places to meet fellow Netheads, they are also a good place to check out different Internet services before you decide which one you like best. Many of the cafés also offer classes in using the Internet or creating a home page, and events for people who have met on-line. And, of course, they are great places for a F2F (face-to-face) meeting with your cyberbeau.

To find one in your area, visit the Cyber Café Guide Web site at www.cyberiacafe.net/cyberia/guide/ccafe.html. At www.cyber-star.com, you'll find the Web site of the International Association of Cybercafés, should you decide to go trotting around the globe.

ARIZONA
Cyber Cafe
1520 South Milton Avenue
Flagstaff, AZ 86001
520-774-0005

Almost Paradise Cafe
4148 1/2 Viking Way
Long Beach, CA 90808
310-429-2066

CALIFORNIA
Al Cappuccino Coffee House
1327 South Harbor
Boulevard
Fullerton, CA 92832
714-870-7588

Cafe Cybernet
8657 Villa La Jolla Drive
La Jolla, CA 92037
619-452-1600

CoffeeNet
744 Harrison Street
San Francisco, CA 94107
415-495-7447

CoffeeTopia
3701 Portola Drive
Santa Cruz, CA 95062
408-477-1940

CyberJava
1029 Abbot Kinney
   Boulevard
Los Angeles, CA 90291
310-581-1300

Cyberworld
528 Folsom Street
San Francisco, CA 94105
415-278-9669

Coffee Bean & Tea Leaf
1835 Newport Boulevard
Costa Mesa, CA 92627
714-722-9673

Cyber House
1407 E. Los Angeles Avenue
Unit G
Simi Valley, CA 93065
805-581-6331

E Cafe
1219 State Street
Santa Barbara, CA 93101
805-897-3335

Gig@Bites
6024 Paseo Delicias
Rancho Sante Fe, CA 92067
619-756-1990

Internet Alfredo
790-A Brannan Street
San Francisco, CA 94103
415-437-3140

Lordsburg Coffee & Tea
2232-D Street
La Verne, CA 91750
909-593-1188

Surf Net Cafe
1445 Donlon Street, #14
Ventura, CA 93003
805-658-1287

World Cafe
2820 Main Street
Santa Monica, CA 90405
310-399-6964

COLORADO
Majordomo's Net Cafe
1401 Ogden Street
Denver, CO 80218
303-830-0442

FLORIDA
Cafe Kaldi
1568 Main Street
Sarasota, FL 34236
941-366-2326

Cafe Internet
12536 Southwest 88th Street
Miami, FL 33186
305-412-0100

Cyber Central Cafe
3924 Cleveland Avenue
Fort Myers, FL 33901
941-274-3064

Jacs Cyber Cafe
1975 Wells Road
Orange Park, FL 32073
904-276-3322

IDAHO
Cyberplayce
7079 Overland Road
Boise, ID 83709
208-377-8701

Metropolis Bakery Cafe
125 Main Avenue East
Twin Falls, ID 83301
208-734-4457

ILLINOIS
Cegab Cyber Cafe
6950 Archer Avenue
Chicago, IL 60638
773-229-0820

The Interactive Bean
1137 Belmont Street
Chicago, IL 60657
773-528-2881

Timber Creek Internet Cafe
15 S. Park Avenue
Lombard, IL 60148
630-268-0559

IOWA
Loft Souls
3510 Cottage Grove
Des Moines, IA 50311
515-279-5639

MASSACHUSETTS
Cybersmith
42 Church Street
Cambridge, MA 02138
617-492-5857

Designs for Living
52 Queensberry Street
Boston, MA 02215
617-536-6150

Internet Cafe
2 Union Street
Nantucket Island, MA 02554
508-228-6777

Sheffield Pub
223 Main Street
Sheffield, MA 01257
413-229-8880

MINNESOTA
Cahoots Coffee Bar
1562 Selby Avenue
St. Paul, MN 55104
612-644-6778

MICHIGAN
Big Surf Cyber Cafe
750 S. Woodward Avenue
Birmingham, MI 48009
810-433-3744

Four Friends Coffee House
& Cyber Lounge
136 Monroe Center
Grand Rapids, MI 49503
616-456-5356

MISSOURI
The Grind
56 Maryland Plaza
St. Louis, MO 63108
314-454-0202

Soho Geek Force
3137 South Grand Street
St. Louis, MO 63118
314-776-6160

MONTANA
Cyber Shack
821 South Higgins Avenue
Missoula, MT 59801
406-721-6251

NEVADA
Cyber City Cafe
Maryland Parkway and
  Flamingo
Las Vegas, NV 89104
702-732-2001

NEW JERSEY
Internet Cafe
One W. Front Street
Red Bank, NJ 07701
732-842-4503

NEW YORK
alt.coffee Inc.
139 Avenue A
New York, NY 10009
212-529-2233

Cafe Connect
125 Jericho Turnpike
Jericho, NY 11753
516-333-6593

Cafe Connect
1441 Old Northern
Boulevard
Roslyn, NY 11576
516-484-6730

Common Grounds Internet
  Cafe
1420 Millersport Highway
Buffalo, NY 14221
716-688-2233

Cyber Cafe Inc.
273 Lafayette Street
New York, NY 10012
212-334-5140

Cyberfelds at the Village
  Copier
20 E. 13th Street
New York, NY 10003
212-647-8830

Cyberweb Cafe
165 European Bank Plaza
Uniondale, NY 11556
516-522-2513

The Internet Cafe
82 E. Third Street
New York, NY 10003
212-614-0747

Kokobar
59 Lafayette Street
Brooklyn, NY 11217
718-243-9040

Wright On Line Internet
  Access Cafe
38 Montauk Highway
Blue Point, NY 11716
516-363-6666

NORTH CAROLINA
Coffee Driade
1215A E. Franklin Street
Chapel Hill, NC 27514
919-933-4161

Cup @Joe
2109-142 Avent Ferry Road
Raleigh, NC 27606
919-828-9886

Escape Computer Center
431-J Western Boulevard
Jacksonville, NC 28546
910-347-2800

OHIO
Web Site Cafe
811 Bethel Road
Columbus, Ohio 43214
614-459-0443

OKLAHOMA
Cyber Hall
215 East Main Street
Norman, OK 73069
405-364-0101

OREGON
Paper Moon Espresso Cafe
11 North First Street
Ashland, OR 97520
541-488-4883

Cyber Cafe
12430 Southwest Main Street
Tigard, OR 97223
503-968-7728

PENNSYLVANIA
CyberLoft
1525 Walnut Street
Philadelphia, PA 19102
215-564-4380

TENNESSEE
Bean Central
2817 West End Avenue
Nashville, TN 37203
615-321-8530

TEXAS
Half Price Books
5525 South Padre Island
 Drive
Moore Plaza
Corpus Christi, TX 78411
512-991-4494

WASHINGTON
Higashi Kaze
623 North Callow
Bremerton, WA 98312
360-377-4170

Speakeasy Cafe
2304 Second Avenue
Seattle, WA 98121
206-728-9770

WISCONSIN
Cyber Zone Cafe
1506 Cleveland Avenue
Marinette, WI 54143
715-732-8500

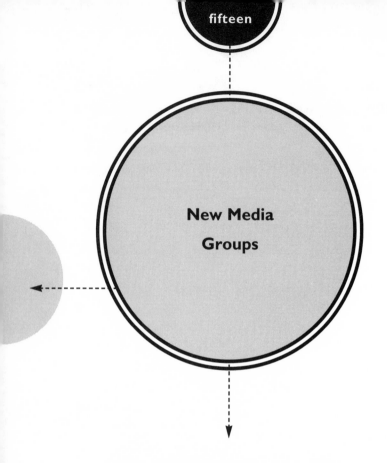

fifteen

New Media

Groups

HOW TO NETWORK YOUR BRAINS OUT

In the interest of turning off your computer and getting out of the house from time to time, you might want to check out the new media associations in your area that hold regular meetings for people involved with computers and the Net. The ratio of men to women at these schmoozefests is about the same as the on-line gender ratio, so it's worth a visit. Here are a few around the country:

The New York New Media Association holds free monthly networking receptions called Cybersuds, which are purely social events. Call 212-459-4649 for more information, or visit www.nynma.org.

The Fairfield County (Connecticut) New Media Association meets once a month. The first part of the evening is spent socializing followed by an Internet-related presentation. For more info, call 203-227-7647, or visit www.townline.com/fcnma.

The New Media Association of New Jersey has free monthly networking parties called CyberPubs. Call 201-267-4200, ext. 193 for the schedule, or E-mail newmedia@nmanj.com.

The Massachusetts Software Council has frequent events including the Interactive Media Forum, which is more of a social group. Although many of the council's meetings are geared to senior executives, the Forum, which is geared to Web designers and other hands-on Netheads, sponsors informational discussions that continue at a local bar. For information, call 617-437-0600, or visit the Web sites www.swcouncil.org and www.icegroup.com.

The Association for Interactive Media is an umbrella organization of new media companies that sponsors networking receptions in Washington, D.C. Call 202-408-0008 for more info.

The International Interactive Communications Society, a worldwide group of new media professionals, is primarily a networking organization. Its Los Angeles chapter is one of the most active. There are several special-interest groups that meet several times a month, so there are up to six events to choose from. Call 310-313-5664 for more information, or visit the Web site at www.laiics.org. **The Los Angeles New Media Roundtable,** better known as LAwNMR (pronounced lawn-mower), is a similar organization. Call their events hotline at 310-535-3388.

The San Francisco Multimedia Development Group has monthly networking meetings that kick off as socials with refreshments. For information, call 415-764-2967.

Last Saturdays is an ongoing gathering of professionals in the new media industry with approximately 9,000 members. Events include lively, roundtable discussions about the effects of new technologies on individuals, communities, and businesses. Despite its name, Last Saturdays members meet on Wednesdays. Go figure. Started by a comedy club owner turned entrepreneur, the group also has chapters in Boston, Chicago, and Austin. For more information, visit www. lastsaturdays.com or E-mail lastsat@aol.com.

Webgrrls is a networking organization for women only (and a nonthreatening way to learn about the Net or swap war stories about cyberdating). "Webgrrls isn't just about the Web," says Aliza Sherman, president of the Cybergrrl, Inc. in New York. "We've created a weblike network of women who get together through E-mail or in our face-to-face meetings to share information." Webgrrls has 100 chapters in various cities, including New York, Boston, Washington, D.C., San Francisco, Denver, Seattle, Toronto, Tokyo, and Wellington, New Zealand. For more info on Webgrrls, visit www.webgrrls.com.